CURRENCY

This chart provides a scale of prices converted from GB pounds, based on a conversion rate of $1.45 to the pound

£1	$1.45
£5	$7.25
£10	$14.50
£20	$29.00
£25	$36.25
£50	$72.50
£75	$108.75
£100	$145.00
£125	$181.25
£150	$217.50
£175	$253.75
£200	$290.00
£250	$362.50
£300	$435.00
£400	$580.00
£500	$725.00
£750	$1,087.50
£1,000	$1,450.00
£2,000	$2,900.00
£5,000	$7,250.00
£7,500	$10,875.00
£10,000	$14,500.00
£20,000	$29,000.00
£30,000	$43,500.00
£40,000	$58,000.00
£50,000	$72,500.00
£100,000	$145,000.00

ANTIQUES COLLECTABLES

THIS IS A CARLTON BOOK

Copyright © 2002 Martin Miller

This edition published by Carlton Books Ltd 2002
20 Mortimer Street
London
W1T 3JW

This book is sold subject to the condition that it shall not, by way of trade or otherwise, be lent, resold, hired out or otherwise circulated without the publisher's prior written consent in any form of cover or binding other than that in which it is published and without a similar condition including this condition, being imposed upon the subsequent purchaser.

All rights reserved.

ISBN 1 84222 540 5

Printed and bound in Italy

ANTIQUES COLLECTABLES

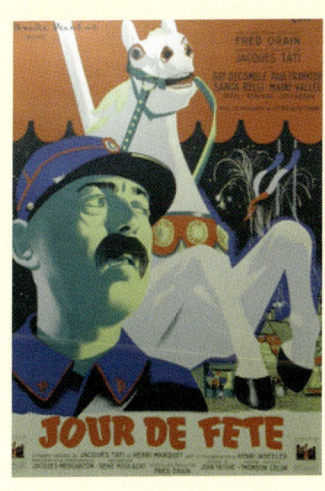

MARTIN MILLER

CONTENTS

Acknowledgements	6
How to Use This Book	7
Introduction	9
Advertising & Packaging	11
Aeronautica	16
Bicycles	18
Bottles	19
Cameras	24
Chess Sets	30
Commemorative Ware	34
Coins & Medals	40
Ephemera	43
Kitchenalia	53
Luggage	63
Mechanical Music	65
Miscellaneous	68
Paperweights	72
Photographs	74
Posters	81
Radio, TV & Sound Equipment	86
Rock & Pop	89
Scripophilly & Paper Money	96
Sewing Items	101
Snuff Boxes & Smoking Equipment	104
Telephones	107
Walking Sticks	112
Directory of Dealers	114
Index	120

ACKNOWLEDGEMENTS

GENERAL EDITOR
Martin Miller

EDITORS
Simon Blake
Marianne Blake
Abigail Zoe Martin
Peter Blake

EDITORIAL CO-ORDINATORS
Marianne Blake
Abigail Zoe Martin

PHOTOGRAPHIC/PRODUCTION
CO-ORDINATOR
Marianne Blake

PHOTOGRAPHERS
Abigail Zoe Martin
James Beam Van Etten
Anna Malni
Chris Smailes
Carmen Klammer

How to Use This Book

by MARTIN MILLER

Due to the phenomenal success of my annual *Antiques Source Book*, we are now producing a series of specialist handbooks, each concentrating on a specific area of buying and collecting antiques and collectables.

Antiques: Collectables is a full-colour collectable retail price guide. The reason that it stands out from other such price guides is that we have used retailers, rather than auction houses, as our sources of information. Many of the items in this book are for sale at the time of going to press and a number, certainly some of the more arcane, will remain so for the lifespan of the book.

A reputable and experienced dealer's assessment of the price of an antique is at least as reliable – and usually a great deal more reasoned – than a price achieved at auction, and so even when the item you wish to purchase from the book turns out to have been sold, you have a reliable guide to the price you should pay when you happen upon another.

This book is designed for maximum visual interest and appeal. It can be treated as a 'through read' as well as a tool for dipping in and out of. The Contents and Index will tell you in which area to find anything which you are specifically seeking.

Should you happen upon something that you wish to buy, simply note the dealer reference to the bottom right of the entry and look up the dealer's full name and details in the Directory of Dealers section towards the back of the book. You can telephone, fax and often visit the dealer's website. All the dealers who have helped us with the book will be happy to assist you and, if the piece you wish to buy has already been sold, they will almost certainly be able to help you find another. Should you wish to sell an item, the relevant section and dealer reference will again be of help, but do not expect to be offered the same price at which the dealer is selling. We all have to make a living!

Good luck and happy hunting!

Introduction

The important rule for the collector of 'collectables' is to take care of the ephemera of today – they may be the antiques of tomorrow.

The way in which antiques are viewed and valued is constantly changing. The distinction, for instance, between 'antique', 'collectable' and 'second-hand' has become very fuzzy in recent years. Curiously, in this disposable age – or perhaps because so much is disposable – the artefacts of today are valued much more by modern collectors than their equivalents were by previous generations, who generally considered that anything owned by their parents was, prima facie, not worth having.

It's an old but true saying that what one throws away today is the collectable of tomorrow. From the soap packet to the mobile phone, all have their place in the collector's market. But watch out for the fads that hit the market with a splash and are just as soon forgotten, such as the Yo-Yo.

The most collectable items are those which are in some ways groundbreaking or revolutionary at the time: for example, radios, TVs or telephones. It is also worth collecting items which are gradually becoming obsolete in the new digital age, for instance records or tapes. Self-winding watches are also a good example of this as very few are currently being made and so their value is rising. It is not too difficult to spot the collectables of the future using this as a criterion – what about the first truly mobile phones, or laptop computers?

The best advice for building a collection is to start with something you have a great personal interest in; this could range from the everyday to the extremely expensive piece. The collector's market is very unpredictable but can be extremely rewarding if you are lucky enough to have chosen that forgotten item that defines the period in which it was made.

The great advantages with collectables is that they do not need to be especially old and they do not need to cost a great deal of money. Take almost any disposable item commonly in use at the moment, and you can be certain that someone is building a collection of it and that, in a few years, it will be much in demand.

Start gathering the antiques of tomorrow today!

Advertising & Packaging

Shop Sign
- *1940s*

A wrought iron shop sign, with scrolled decoration surrounding a clover leaf emblem with the hand-painted letters "Sunshine Bakery". In original condition.
- *102cm x 65cm*
- £220
- Old School

Dresden Figurine
- *1910*

A Dresden porcelain group of figures advertising Yardley perfumes and soaps.
- *height 17cm*
- £350
- Huxtable's

Packet of Condoms
- *1950s*

An assortment of 1950s condoms.
- *16cm x 5cm/packet*
- £10
- Huxtable's

Manufacturer's Sign
- *1930s*

A sign cut from hardwood of the figure of John Bull, advertising John Bull Tyres.
- *height 65cm*
- £120
- Huxtable's

Ink Bottle
- *1930s*

A bottle of blue black Swan ink.
- *height 8cm*
- £6
- Huxtable's

Advertising & Packaging

Boat Biscuit Box
- circa 1935
A French biscuit box in the shape of the ill-fated liner, *Normandie*.
- length 62cm
- £350
- Huxtable's

Guinness Print
- circa 1950
Showing a pint glass and smiling face with famous slogan: "Guinness Is Good For You".
- 78cm x 50cm
- £14
- Magpies

Queen of Hearts Box
- circa 1920
A sweet box from *Alice in Wonderland* in the shape of Tenniel's Queen of Hearts.
- height 20cm
- £75
- Huxtable's

Salt Cellar
- circa 1950
A Sifta glass salt cellar with a bakelite top.
- height 9cm
- £4.50
- Magpies

Cocoa Tin
- circa 1920
A Dutch cocoa tin from Bendorp's Cocoa, Amsterdam.
- height 9cm
- £20
- Huxtable's

Cigarette Sign
- circa 1920
A Craven "A" advertising sign in blue, white and red, including one of advertising's great lies.
- height 92cm
- £28
- Magpies

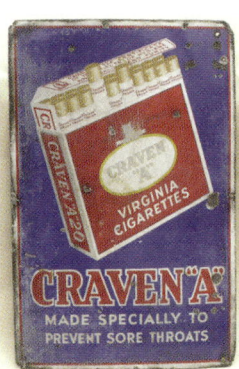

Wills's Star Cigarettes
- circa 1920
An enamelled point-of-sale sign in brown and orange.
- height 28cm
- £42
- Magpies

Advertising and Packaging

Lux Soap Flakes
- *circa 1960*
An unopened box of Lever Brothers' Lux soap flakes.
- *height 28cm*
- £10
- Huxtable's

Toothpaste Lid
- *circa 1900*
A Woods Areca Nut toothpaste lid by W. Woods, Plymouth.
- £20
- Magpies

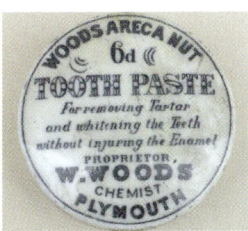

Biscuit Tin
- *circa 1910*
A biscuit tin in the shape of a book, made by Hoffman Suisse.
- *height 36cm*
- £90
- Huxtable's

McVitie Biscuit Box
- *circa 1910*
A "Billie Bird" biscuit box by McVitie.
- *height 32cm*
- £120
- Huxtable's

Talcum Powder
- *circa 1950*
A "Jolly Baby" talcum powder container, with voluptuous cover.
- *height 15cm*
- £40
- Huxtable's

Horlicks Mixer
- *circa 1950*
A Horlicks promotional glass jug with a metal mixer.
- *height 15cm*
- £10
- Magpies

Battery Advertisement
- *circa 1960*
An Oldham Batteries metal advertising sign, incorporating the "I told 'em – Oldham" slogan.
- *height 37cm*
- £28
- Magpies

13

Advertising & Packaging

Bottle of Broseden
- *1930s*
A bottle of "Broseden" made in Germany. A drink used to calm the troops during lonely times.
- *height 9cm*
- £5
- Huxtable's

Bournvita Mug
- *1950s*
A white Bournvita mug in the shape of a face with a blue nightcap and a red pom-pom. With large handle.
- *height 14cm*
- £40
- Huxtable's

Toffee Tin
- *20th century*
A Macintosh's toffee tin commemorating the marriage of George VI to Elizabeth Bowes-Lyon.
- *diameter 14cm*
- £20
- Huxtable's

Brilliantine
- *1930s*
A glass bottle of "Saturday Night Lotion", men's hair styling gloss.
- *height 13cm*
- £12
- Huxtable's

Carton of Cigarettes
- *1960s*
A carton of Senior Service cigarettes. In original white paper wrapping with navy blue lettering, unopened.
- *13cm x 5cm*
- £40
- Huxtable's

Nib Boxes
- *1920s*
An assortment of unopened nib boxes.
- *width 7cm*
- £7
- Huxtable's

Advertising & Packaging

Guinness Trays
- *circa 1950*

A metal drinks tray with a toucan holding the advertisement for Guinness.
- *diameter 16cm*
- £50
- Huxtable's

Guinness Toucan
- *1955*

A toucan with a glass of Guinness on a stand advertising the beer with the slogan –
"My goodness – my Guinness".
- *height 7cm*
- £250
- Huxtable's

Dog Food Sign
- *1950*

A Spratt's wooden sign advertising dog food with the picture of a Highland terrier in the form of the word "Spratts".
- *50cm x 80cm*
- £100
- Huxtable's

Lollipop Man
- *1960s*

A porcelain figure of a Robertson's Golly Lollipop Man.
- *height 12cm*
- £12
- Huxtable's

Guinness Tray
- *circa 1950*

Circular tray advertising Guinness.
- £50
- Huxtable's

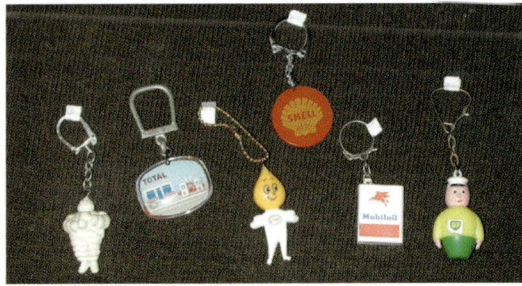

Mustard Tins
- *1930s*

An assortment of Coleman's mustard tins. Decorated with red writing and the Union Jack on a yellow background.
- *height 12cm*
- £7
- Huxtable's

Motoring Key Rings
- *1960s*

Assortment of motoring key rings.
- £10
- Huxtable's

Trumps Markers
- *1930s*

Two trumps markers for use in card games.
- £20
- Huxtable's

Aeronautica

BOAC Sales Leaflet
- *circa 1970*
Advertising standard merchandise of the era. With colour pictures.
- length 20cm
- £10
- Cobwebs

Model Kit
- *circa 1940*
"Robot Bomb" balsa-wood model of a jet-propelled bomb used against England by the Germans in France during World War II.
- £10
- Cobwebs

Aero Club Badge
- *circa 1920*
Brooklands club badge in pressed steel with coloured enamels. The club was established in the 1920s.
- height 10cm
- £600
- CARS

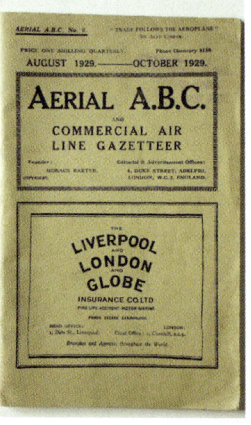

Aerial ABC Gazetteer
- **August 1929**
Light brown in colour with black and white print. In mint condition.
- 22cm x 14.5cm
- £40
- Cobwebs

Spanish Airline Leaflet
- *circa 1922*
In good condition, but with a folding crease down the centre.
- 15.5cm x 12cm
- £25
- Cobwebs

Fighter Plane Model
- *circa 1980*
Model of a battle-camouflaged Tornado fighter plane. On a steel frame with rubber feet.
- height 10cm
- £30
- Cobwebs

Expert Tips

The most enduringly collectable aeronautical artefacts tend still to be those of World War II and, most particularly, those relating to the Battle of Britain, 1940.

Qantas Empire Airways
- *circa 1930*
A Qantas flying-boat map of the Sydney to Singapore route. Good condition.
- length 24.5cm, width 12cm
- £50
- Cobwebs

Aeronautica

Airship Safety Award
- *circa 1959*
An American "Aviation Safety Award" with brass engraving set in a plaque of beechwood.
- *16cm x 13cm*
- £25-30
- Cobwebs

Aircraft Propellor
- *circa 1920*
A four-bladed wooden coarse-pitched, wind-generator propeller, in mahogany with lamination and holes in the centre intact.
- *length 61cm*
- £165
- Cobwebs

Souvenir Programme
- *1930*
Illustrated souvenir programme from the British Hospitals' Air Pageant, 1930. In good condition.
- *21.5cm x 14cm*
- £40
- Cobwebs

Aerial Timetable
- *1927*
"International Aerial Time Table" in good condition and in colour print, with a fascinating cover picture of unlikely flyers.
- *21.5cm x 14cm*
- £50
- Cobwebs

> **Expert Tips**
>
> Early aerospace companies were nearly as prolific in their day as dot.com companies today. The merchandising materials of these long-dead organisations often fetch a fortune.

Promotional Magazine
- *circa 1917*
Whitehead aircraft company promotional magazine. In good condition with black and white and colour prints.
- *19cm x 12cm*
- £30
- Cobwebs

Model Airplane
- *circa 1940*
Chrome model, twin-engined unidentified American plane.
- *height 10cm*
- £65
- Cobwebs

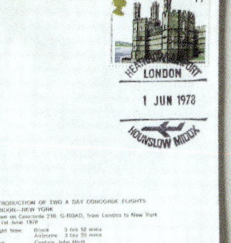

Concorde Postal Cover
- *circa 1978*
Commemorating the first flight from London to New York, with colour print showing an early Concorde in blue sky.
- *19cm x 11.5cm*
- £15
- Cobwebs

Bicycles

Bicycles

Arnold Schwin Parckard ▶
- *circa 1930*
American lady's bicycle, with pedal back brake, maroon finish, single-speed. Very good condition.
- *66cm wheel*
- £550
- Bridge Bikes

Raleigh Roadster ▲
- *circa 1950*
Single-speed post-war bike. Good rideable condition, with Westwood rims and rod brakes.
- *66cm wheel*
- £50
- G Whizz

Expert Tips

There is no doubt that fear for the ozone layer and the increasing vilification of the motorcar has led to an upsurge in the popularity of the bicycle. They need to be in good condition and working.

Raleigh Rocky II ▶
- *1986*
Raleigh Rocky II with fifteen Shimano gears.
- *153cm frame*
- *66cm wheel*
- £200
- G Whizz

Italian Legnano ▲
- *circa 1940*
Lady's cycle, single-speed, unique rod brakes running through handlebars, full chain cover.
- *66cm wheel*
- £100
- Bridge Bikes

Humber Gents ▼
- *circa 1940*
Gent's bike with enclosed chain, three-speed hub, rod brake.
- *156cm frame*
- *71cm wheel*
- £150
- Bridge Bikes

Rival of Norwich ◀
- *circa 1930*
Lady's roadster. Unusual make and very collectable.
- *155cm seat tube*
- *63cm wheel*
- £50
- G Whizz

Bottles

Silver Scent Bottle
- *circa 1886*
An English, decorative silver scent bottle with scrolls and a cut-glass stopper.
- *height 5.5cm*
- £250 • John Clay

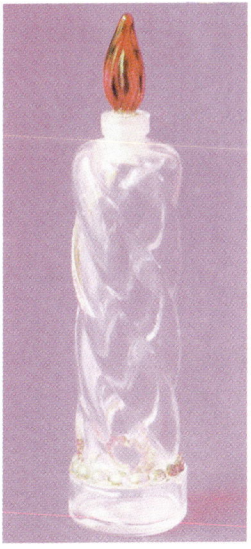

Schiaparelli Bottle
- *circa 1938*
A Schiaparelli perfume bottle of twisted and fluted design with red finial top and beaded base.
- £180 • Linda Bee

Saville London "June"
- *circa 1930*
A novelty perfume bottle in the form of a sundial.
- £125 • Linda Bee

French Glass Perfume
- *1860*
Mazarin blue glass perfume bottle with floral gilding and large octagonal stopper.
- *height 16cm*
- £145 • Trio

European Perfume
- *1880*
Perfume bottle of latissimo glass with engraved silver cover with glass stopper inside.
- £190 • Trio

Prince Matchabello "Beloved"
- *circa 1950*
Enamel crown bottle. With inner and outer box.
- £220 • Linda Bee

Bourjois Kobako
- *circa 1925*
A fashionable oriental-style perfume bottle, designed by Bourjois of Paris, with bakelite cover and carved stand.
- £390 • Linda Bee

Guerlain "L'Heure Bleue" ▼
- circa 1940
Made by Baccarate perfume, with original box.
- £125
- Linda Bee

Grossmith "Old Cottage" Lavender Water ▲
- circa 1930
A bottle of English lavender water of etched glass.
- £95
- Linda Bee

Nina Ricci "Coeur-Joie" ▼
- 1946
Lalique bottle with heart-shaped centre and floral decoration.
- £210
- Linda Bee

Conical Bottle ▼
- circa 1866
A mid-Victorian silver fluted perfume bottle, of conical form, with silver stopper.
- £210
- Trio

Bohemian Glass Bottle ▲
- circa 1860
Floral perfume bottle, in Bohemian glass, with enamelling and large cut stopper.
- £300
- Trio

Unknown Heart-Shaped Perfume Bottle ▼
- circa 1940
With etched glass and bakelite base with dipper.
- £65
- Linda Bee

French Apothecary's Bottles ▶
- 19th century
Collection of nine apothecary's bottles including stoppers.
- £655 set
- Ranby Hall

Bottles

Circular Scent Bottle
- 1902
A circular scent bottle painted with two Japanese ladies in traditional dress embracing each other, set against a background of green foliage.
- *diameter 7cm*
- £155   • Trio

Square Scent Bottle
- *circa 1890*
A square French scent bottle in turquoise, fitted with a gold stopper and chain. Decorated with a gold floral design.
- *diameter 3cm*
- £158   • Trio

Oval Scent Bottle
- *circa 1890*
An oval, Victorian scent bottle in white porcelain, with a silver stopper. Decorated with a red butterfly, pink flowers and foliage.
- *height 6cm*
- £158   • Trio

Expert Tips

When examining a bottle, make sure that the glass is in a non-chipped state and is devoid of cracks. If there are chips on the rim these can sometimes be ground out.

Enamel Scent Bottle
- *circa 1890*
A white enamel scent bottle decorated with pink flowers and surmounted by filigree work on a gold chain.
- *diameter 3cm*
- £135   • Trio

Victorian Scent Bottle
- *circa 1890*
A Victorian, oval scent bottle in clear glass, decorated with gold flowers and fitted with a pinch-back gold chain.
- *height 6cm*
- £199   • Trio

Bottles

Bohemian Glass Bottle
- *circa 1860*
Floral perfume bottle and large cut stopper in Bohemian glass, with enamelling.
- £300
- Trio

Square Scent Bottle
- *1930*
Square glass Art Deco perfume bottle, with a clear glass stopper and large grey silk tassel. Decorated with a black floral design.
- height 10cm
- £138
- Trio

Heart-Shaped Porcelain Bottle
- *circa 1906*
A heart-shaped porcelain scent bottle, with a silver stopper. Decorated with a pair of eighteenth century figures.
- diameter 4cm
- £178
- Trio

Red Glass Scent Bottle
- *1920*
Art Deco perfume bottle in deep red glass, with a tassel and opaque glass stopper.
- height 14cm
- £168
- Trio

Jug-Shaped Scent Bottle
- *1860*
A French ruby scent bottle in the shape of a stylised jug, with ruby stopper. Decorated with a gilt foliage design on the bottle and handle. The metal base carries a gilt foliage design.
- height 12cm
- £210
- Trio

Bottles

Silver-Topped Bottle
- *Georgian*
An early Georgian opaque scent bottle with silver top.
- height 11cm
- £178   • Trio

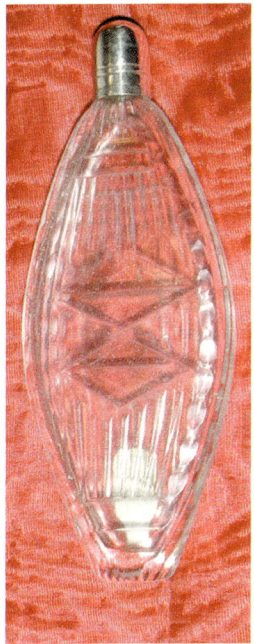

Stoneware Bottle
- circa 1647
Whit stoneware bottle of bulbous proportions with handle, on a splayed base, inscribed with the words, "WHIT, 1647".
- height 6cm
- N/A   • Jonathan Horne

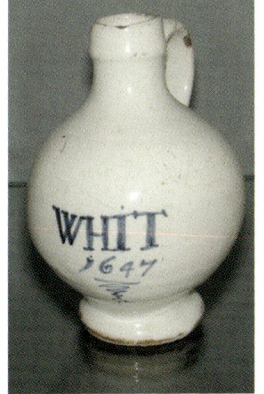

Victorian Scent Bottles
- 1880
Two Victorian cranberry- and vaseline-coloured scent bottles, together with their original leather carrying case.
- height 14cm
- £245   • Trio

Clear Glass Bottle
- circa 1870
A clear glass scent bottle elaborately decorated with ornate pinch beck. The stopper is painted with a scene of Church Street, Magdalene.
- height 7.5cm
- £188   • Trio

English Scent Bottle
- 1920
English salmon-pink Art Deco perfume bottle, styled in the shape of a sailing boat with sail.
- height 14cm
- £150   • Trio

Green Scent Bottle
- circa 1890
Green simulated vaseline glass scent bottle decorated with red and gold filigree with opaque glass stopper.
- height 12cm
- £110   • Trio

Cameras

Reflex Camera
- *circa 1960*
Rolleiflex 2.8f twin lens reflex camera with built-in light meter and overhead viewfinder.
- £600
- Jessop Classic Photographica

Kodak Field Camera
- *circa 1950*
Kodak No.1 Autographic 120mm film field camera with folding case.
- £70
- Mac's Cameras

35mm SLR Camera
- *circa 1965*
Leicaflex 35mm SLR with f/2 semi-micron lens.
- £400
- Mac's Cameras

Expert Tips

The Leica camera totally dominated the 35mm market from the mid-1920s until the 1960s. Virtually any Leica camera will sell well at auction, the most avid collectors being the Japanese.

Cine Camera
- *circa 1960*
Bell & Howell "Sportster Standard 8" 8mm cine camera.
- £30
- Mac's Cameras

Filma Projector
- *circa 1970*
Filma 240f 8mm sound projector. Standard 8 sound and silent. Portable and with outfit case.
- £100
- Mac's Cameras

Rollei Camera
- *circa 1975*
Rollei 35S gold 35mm camera. A specially finished precision compact camera. Limited edition of 1500, gold-plated.
- £900
- Jessop Classic Photographica

Field Camera
- *circa 1930*
Deardorff 10x8-inch camera made of mahogany with nickel-plated fittings. Schneider and Symmar 300mm lens.
- £2,000
- Jessop Classic Photographica

Cameras

Purma Roll Camera
- circa 1932
Purma "Special" bakelite 127 roll camera with telescoping lens.
- £30
- Jessop Classic Photographica

Leicaflex SLR Camera
- circa 1970
Leicaflex 35mm SLR camera with f2.8/90 Elmarit lens.
- £500
- Mac's Cameras

Hollywood Splicer
- circa 1960
Hollywood stainless-steel splicer. 8mm x 16mm, in original box.
- £30
- Mac's Cameras

Flash-Bulb Holder
- circa 1949
Leica Chico flash-bulb holder for Leica cameras.
- £20
- Jessop Classic Photographica

Mamiya 120 Camera
- circa 1970–1980
Mamiya C33 first professional 120 camera with interchangeable lens. 6x6 image.
- £170
- Mac's Cameras

Expert Tips
Mint condition boxed originals are worth about double the price of the same camera showing reasonable wear. But the latter must be in perfect working order.

Roll Film Camera
- circa 1935
Coronet midget 16mm camera made in five colours, blue being the rarest. Made in Birmingham.
- £350
- Jessop Classic Photographica

Miniature Spy Camera
- circa 1958
Minox B sub miniature spy camera, which takes 8x11mm negatives. With brushed aluminium body.
- £180
- Jessop Classic Photographica

Cameras

Light Exposure Meter ▶
- *circa 1960*
- 1 Kophot light exposure meter by Zeiss in a folding burgundy leather case.
- £30
- Mac's Cameras

Pyramid Tripod ▶
- *circa 1960*
- Camera base with wooden legs and adjustable tubular metal stands.
- £15
- Mac's Cameras

Field Camera ▲
- *circa 1954*
- MPP micro precision 5x4 press camera. Made in Kingston-upon-Thames, Surrey.
- £300
- Jessop Classic Photographica

Robot Camera ▲
- *circa 1940*
- Luftwaffen Eigentum German Airforce robot camera. With built-in clockwork spring motor.
- £300
- Jessop Classic Photographica

Brownie Box Camera ▼
- *circa 1960*
- Brownie Box camera, for 127 film, made in Canada by Kodak Eastman Co Ltd.
- £30
- Mac's Cameras

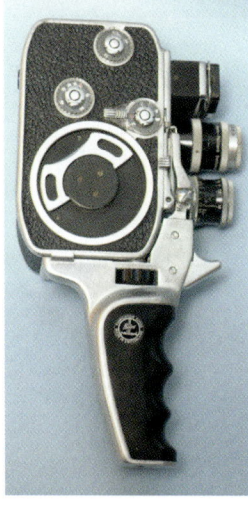

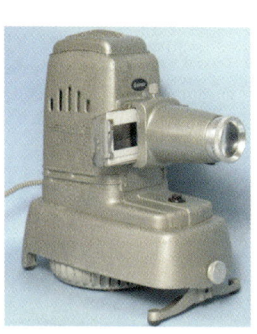

Cine Camera ▲
- *circa 1960*
- A standard 8 film Bolex 8mm cine camera and a selection of Kern lenses with leather cases and original instructions.
- £100
- Mac's Cameras

Slide Projector ▲
- *circa 1960*
- Aldis 35mm slide projector with original box.
- £30
- Mac's Cameras

Expert Tips

George Eastman's invention of the dry plate, in 1879, led to the mass production of cameras. The first Box Brownie was produced in 1888 and they changed almost imperceptibly for 80 years.

Cameras

Quarter-Plate Camera
- *circa 1935*
Baby speed graphic quarter plate camera. Made in America. With original leather straps.
- £400
- Jessop Classic Photographica

Autographic Camera
- *circa 1920*
A Kodak vest pocket Autographic camera. Made in Rochester NY, USA.
- £30
- Mac's Cameras

Meopta Cine Camera
- *circa 1958–65*
A standard 8 Meopta Admira 8mm cine camera with full metal case.
- £30
- Mac's Cameras

Mickey Mouse Camera
- *circa 1980*
A 110 cartridge system camera with a plastic body in the form of Mickey Mouse. With viewfinder placed on forehead.
- £50
- Jessop Classic Photographica

Brownie 'Flash' Camera
- *circa 1970*
A Brownie 'flash' 20 camera with interchangeable flash. With built-in filters. All plastic body in very good condition.
- £30
- Mac's Cameras

Expert Tips

Wet-plate cameras were manufactured from 1840–90 and are very rare. The craftsmanship of the case, as well as the manufacturer's name, define the value.

Square Roll Film Camera
- *circa 1953*
First six V 120 6x6cm square roll film camera. One of the first to be made in Japan, inspired by earlier German designs.
- £100
- Jessop Classic Photographica

Cartridge System Camera
- *circa 1975*
A 110 cartridge system camera modelled as a caricature of a British Airways Aeroplane. In good condition.
- £60
- Jessop Classic Photographica

Cameras

Bolex 16mm Cine Camera ▶
- *circa 1960s*
Bolex 16mm cine camera, model number H16m, with a Swiss-made body and Som Berthiot 17–85mm zoom lens.
- *33cm x 21.5cm*
- £500 • Jessop Classic

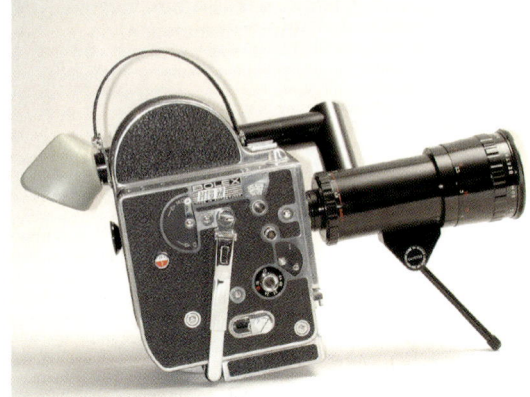

C8 Cine Camera ▼
- *1954*
Bolex Standard 8 cine camera with a clockwork windup and single interchangeable lens.
- *12.5cm x 6cm*
- £50 • Jessop Classic

Thornton Pickard Camera ▲
- *circa 1909*
Triple extension, Thornton Pickard camera which uses ½ plate-sized negatives (glass plates used, not films). Made of wood with leather bellows.
- *21cm x 25.5cm*
- £300 • Jessop Classic

Teleca Bino Camera ▼
- *1950*
Relatively rare, subminiature 16mm Teleca Bino camera, which is built into a pair of binoculars. Fitted with standard 10mm x 14mm lenses and supplied with a brown leather case.
- *10 x 9cm*
- £299 • Photo. Gallery

Widelux Super Wide Angle Camera ▲
- *circa 1970s*
Widelux super wide angle viewfinder camera with an unusual rotating lens. The camera uses 120 film.
- *23cm x 28cm*
- £1,399 • Jessop Classic

Kodak Medallist II Rangefinder Camera ▲
- *1946–53*
Rare Kodak Medallist II rangefinder camera, fitted with an F3.5 100mm Ektar lens.
- *20cm x 13cm*
- £349 • Jessop Classic

Cameras

> ### Expert Tips
> Collecting cameras is not only fun but you also have the bonus that they are usable. SLR cameras are a good future investment, especially with the onset of the digital age.

Rollei 35 Camera ▼
- 1971

Gold Rollei 35 camera, supplied with a brown leather case and a red felt-lined wooden box. Fitted with an F3.5 Tessar lens.
- 9.5cm x 6cm
- £899   • Jessop Classic

Rollei Camera ▲
- 1966–67

Rollei 35 standard camera fitted with an F3.5 Tessar lens.
- 9.5cm x 6cm
- £299   • Jessop Classic

Kodak Retina II F, 35mm Camera ▼
- 1963

Kodak Retina II F, 35mm camera with an F2.8, 45mm Xenar lens. The built-in flash bulb holder is an unusual feature for this style of camera.
- 13cm x 8.5cm
- £100   • Jessop Classic

Canon IV Camera ▲
- circa 1950s

Canon IV range finder camera with detachable flash unit and a 50mm 1.9 Serenar lens. Supplied with a brown leather case. This model is based on a Leica design.
- 14cm x 7cm
- £499   • Jessop Classic

Houghton Ticka Camera ▲
- 1905–14

Houghton Ticka Spy camera. This is designed to look like a pocket watch with an engraved monogram on the cover. The camera is hidden underneath the winding mechanism.
- 6.5cm x 5cm
- £249   • Jessop Classic

Blair Stereo Weno with Case ▶
- 1902

Blair stereo Weno camera with case (as seen underneath), made in Rochester, New York. Supplied with a pair of Plastigmat lenses. Uses 116 Kodak film which has now been discontinued.
- 26.5cm x 11.5cm
- £299   • Jessop Classic

Chess Sets

Ivory Chess Set
- circa 1845
A rare 19th-century French design ivory chess set.
- height 10cm (king)
- £8,500   • G.D. Coleman

Tortoiseshell & Ivory Chess Set
- 19th century
Interlaced vine decoration on light mahogany base.
- height 19cm
- £650   • Shahdad

Boxwood and Ebony Staunton Chess Set
- late 19th century
Mahogany green baize-lined lift-top box with Jacques of London green paper label to the inside lid.
- height 19cm (king)
- £950   • G.D. Coleman

Mythological Chess Set
- circa 1920
Unusual French decorated lead chess set on a mythological classical theme.
- height 13cm (king)
- £1,800   • G.D. Coleman

Painted Metal Chess Set
- circa 1920
King and queen representing mythical gods. White figures show a mottled effect.
- £1,800   • G.D. Coleman

Selenus Chess Set
- circa 1800
German carved bone with red and white kings and queens topped by Maltese crosses.
- height 12cm
- £2,850   • G.D. Coleman

Portuguese European vs Chinese Chess Set
- circa 1865
Fine carved ivory, from Macau.
- height 10cm (king)
- £1,850   • G.D. Coleman

Chess Sets

Quartz Chess Set ◄
- **19th century**
An Indian rock crystal (quartz) export chess set with red and white colours.
- £1,250   • G.D. Coleman

Russian Ivory Chess Set ▼
- **19th century**
Carved and turned in mammoth ivory. One side natural, the other side with unusual pewter effect.
- *height 8.2cm (king)*
- £850   • G.D. Coleman

Staunton Chess Set ▲
- **circa 1880**
Ivory Staunton chess set by Jaques of London with "Carton Pierre" casket and chess board.
- £2,500   • G.D. Coleman

"Bauhaus" Wooden Chess Set ▲
- **early 20th century**
Chess set and board (not photographed).
- *height 10cm (king)*
- £380   • G.D. Coleman

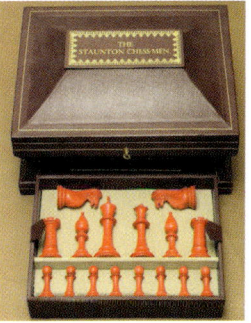

Wooden Chess Set ▼
- **19th century**
Very rare. All pieces are in the form of "The Bears of Berne". Made of Swiss natural wood, some stained darker.
- £2,850   • G.D. Coleman

Expert Tips

The modern era of chess dates from the 16th century, when the moves of the game began to take their present form. Philidor, a Frenchman who played in the 1700s, is widely regarded as the first world champion.

Staunton Ivory Set ▲
- **circa 1865**
Magnificent rare set by Jaques of London. With gold and red leather case and board.
- *height 14cm (king)*
- £16,500   • G.D. Coleman

Ivory Monobloc Set ►
- **circa 1835**
Finely carved. One side in rare stained green, the other natural.
- *height 10.5cm (king)*
- £2,850   • G.D. Coleman

Chess Sets

American Chess Set
- 1876

American chess set in soft metal, signed "Le Mon" and dated 1876. Presented in its original box.
- height 10cm/king
- £3,500
- G.D. Coleman

German Chess Set
- 1795

German chess set of Selenus design, with black and white pieces in ivory.
- height 8cm
- £790
- G.D. Coleman

Coromandel Games Compendium
- circa 1880

Coromandel games box in wood, containing chess, backgammon, checkers, cribbage, dominoes and draughts.
- 33cm x 20cm x 22cm
- £1,900
- Langfords Marine

French Chess Set
- 1800

French chess set with pieces carved from lion wood and bone. Figures are black or red, both colours decorated with white edging.
- height 8cm/king
- £1,650
- G.D. Coleman

Expert Tips

The Victorian era (1837–1901) saw a great expansion in board games, and chess was no exception, and with the expansion of the British Empire pieces can be found from all over the world. The most celebrated designer of chess pieces is Jack Staunton whose work is of the Victorian era, and remains highly collectable.

Military Chess Set
- 1870

Chinese export ivory chess set based on the military theme of the Emperor Napoleon versus the Duke of Wellington.
- height 10cm/king
- £2,450
- G.D. Coleman

Chess Sets

French Ivory Chess Set
- 1800
French ivory chess set, with one side in natural ivory and one side coloured in faded Shagrin green.
- height 9cm/king
- £1,750   • G. D. Coleman

Silver Chess Set
- 1970
English silver and silver gilt chess set of rococo design bearing a hallmark.
- height 9cm/king
- £1,950   • G.D. Coleman

Bone Chess Set
- 1840
English chess set in carved bone, with figures in red and white.
- height 8cm/king
- £1,250   • G.D. Coleman

Expert Tips

It is possible to chart the development of board games from as far back as 5,000 years ago. These games mainly centred around themes of war, competition and chance. This is indicative of the game of chess, and even though its pieces are medieval in character they can actually be created in any shape as it is their interaction which is important. The first chess set came from India but some have been found in Scandinavia dating back to 1,000 AD.

Backgammon and Chess Set
- 1840
Indian ivory chess and backgammon set, with black and natural ivory figures. Presented in folding ivory chessboard box.
- 45cm x 50cm x 5cm
- £4,500   • G.D. Coleman

Staunton Chess Set
- 19th century
Ebony and boxwood chess set made by Staunton, presented in original box, by Jakes of London.
- height 9cm/king
- £480   • G.D. Coleman

Commemorative Ware

Bone China Jug
- 1888

Continental bone china jug commemorating the silver wedding anniversary of Prince Edward and Princess Alexandra.
- height 12.5cm
- £85
- Hope & Glory

Caricature Mug
- 1991

A caricature mug of the former Prime Minister Margaret Thatcher and her husband.
- height 9cm
- £33
- Hope & Glory

Queen Elizabeth II Bust
- 1953

Bust of Queen Elizabeth II to commemorate her coronation in 1953, by Staffordshire Morloy.
- height 18cm
- £80
- Hope & Glory

Golden Jubilee Beaker
- 1887

Beaker commemorating the golden jubilee of Queen Victoria, showing young and old portraits. Issued as a gift to school children in Hyde Park.
- height 10.5cm
- £125
- Hope & Glory

Golden Jubilee Mug
- 1887

Small cream and blue mug, commemorating the golden jubilee of Queen Victoria. Sold in the Isle of Wight.
- height 6cm
- £125
- Hope & Glory

Accession Jug
- 1837

Blue and white Accession jug inscribed "Hail Victoria". Showing a portrait of the young Queen Victoria.
- height 29cm
- £1,275
- Hope & Glory

Commemorative Ware

Coronation Mug
- 1911
Coronation mug of King George V and Queen Mary.
- height 7cm
- £24
- Magpies

Loving Cup
- 1937
A bone china loving cup, by Shelly, to commemorate the proposed coronation of King Edward VIII.
- height 11.5cm
- £275
- Hope & Glory

Poole Pottery Vase
- 1977
Vase commemorating the silver jubilee of Queen Elizabeth II, showing the lion and unicorn.
- height 25cm
- £125
- Hope & Glory

Musical Teapot
- circa 1953
Teapot in the form of a coach, commemorating the coronation of Queen Elizabeth II. Plays the National Anthem.
- height 13cm
- £240
- Hope & Glory

Winston S. Churchill Toby Jug
- circa 1941
With anchor handle, by Fieldings, representing Churchill's second appointment as First Lord.
- height 15cm
- £190
- Hope & Glory

Pottery Mug
- circa 1969
A mug from the Portmerion pottery to commemorate the first landing of men on the moon by Apollo II.
- height 10cm
- £70
- Hope & Glory

Snuffbox
- 1895
Victorian silver table snuffbox, inscribed as presented by HRH Albert Edward of Wales.
- length 14cm
- £2,850
- S. & A. Thompson

35

Commemorative Ware

Four Castles Plate
- 1901
Black transfer on earthenware plate to commemorate the death of Queen Victoria, such items are quite scarce.
- diameter 24.5cm
- £240   • Hope & Glory

Bone China Plate
- circa 1900
By Royal Worcester to commemorate the relief of Mafeking. Transfer shows Baden-Powell.
- diameter 23.5cm
- £140   • Hope & Glory

Victorian Mug
- circa 1878
Mug commemorating the visit of Edward, Prince of Wales, to India on the occasion of Queen Victoria being made Empress.
- height 10.5cm
- £150   • Hope & Glory

Dutch Delft Plaque
- circa 1945
To commemorate the liberation of Holland. Showing mother, child and aeroplane.
- height 20cm
- £150   • Hope & Glory

Chocolate Tin
- circa 1953
Royal blue enamelled tin with fleur de lys motif, commemorating the coronation of Queen Elizabeth II.
- height 7cm
- £5   • Magpies

Expert Tips

The market for commemorative items is driven by emotion. They start off overpriced and, as the individual becomes less well known, may lose value.

Officer on Horseback
- circa 1910
German. Napoleonic period. Probably Dresden.
- height 38cm
- £2,500   • The Armoury

Pottery Loving Cup
- 1897
Loving cup by Brannum pottery, commemorating the Diamond Jubilee of Queen Victoria.
- height 14cm
- £240   • Hope & Glory

Commemorative Ware

Whisky Decanter
- *1911*
Spode decanter made for Andrew Usher & Co, distillers, Edinburgh, commemorating the coronation of George V.
- *height 25cm*
- £160
- Hope & Glory

Pair of Perfume Flasks
- *circa 1840*
Hand-decorated porcelain perfume flasks by Jacob Petit, commemorating the marriage of Queen Victoria and Prince Albert.
- *height 31cm*
- £3,750
- Hope & Glory

Coronation Mug
- *1902*
Copeland mug commemorating the coronation of King Edward VII and Queen Alexandra. This mug shows the correct date of August 9th, 1902. Most commemorative ware gives the date as June 26th, from when the event was postponed due to the King's appendicitis.
- *height 7.5cm*
- £160
- Hope & Glory

Children's Plate
- *1847*
Showing the young Edward, Prince of Wales, on a pony. Entitled "England's Hope".
- *diameter 16.5cm*
- £340
- Hope & Glory

Ceramic Plaque
- *circa 1911*
Plaque, by Ridgways, to commemorate the coronation of George VI and Queen Mary.
- *16 x 21cm*
- £85
- Hope & Glory

Wedgwood Mug
- *circa 1937*
A Wedgwood mug commemorating the coronation of King George VI, designed by Eric Ravilious.
- *height 11cm*
- £475
- Hope & Glory

Teapot
- *circa 1897*
Commemorating the Diamond Jubilee of Queen Victoria. Copeland bone china with gold decoration. Portrait of Victoria in relief.
- *height 14cm*
- £525
- Hope & Glory

Commemorative Ware

Victorian Cypher
- 1890
Victorian English carved wooden gesso royal cypher.
- 90cm x 65cm
- £2,500   • Lacquer Chest

Miners' Strike Plate
- 1984
Bone china plate to commemorate the great miners' strike of 1984–85. Issued by the National Union of Mineworkers.
- diameter 27cm
- £58   • Hope & Glory

Loving Cup
- 1987
Bone china loving cup by Royal Crown Derby. Commemorating the third term in office of Margaret Thatcher. Limited edition of 650.
- height 7.75cm
- £160   • Hope & Glory

Jubilee Mug
- 1935
Ceramic mug celebrating the silver jubilee of King George V and Queen Mary.
- height 7cm
- £24   • Magpies

Engagement Mug
- 1981
China mug depicting Prince Charles's ear. Drawn by Marc Boxer, made at the engagement of Charles and Diana.
- £5   • Hope & Glory

Royal Visit Teapot
- 1939
Teapot issued in commemoration of a royal visit to Canada made by George VI and Queen Elizabeth I in 1939.
- height 13cm
- £85   • Hope & Glory

Expert Tips
The condition of any commemorative ware is just as important as the attractiveness of the item; even so, limited editions considerably enhance the desirability of a piece. Make sure that the transfers are bright and unscratched. In terms of subjects, opt for kings, queens or politicians who ruled for a short time.

Commemorative Ware

Coalport Plate
- 1897
Bone china plate issued by Coalport to commemorate Queen Victoria's diamond jubilee.
- *diameter 22cm*
- £140 • Hope & Glory

Boer War Egg Cups
- 1900
Continental bone china egg cups depicting generals from the Boer War.
- *height 6.5cm*
- £60 each • Hope & Glory

Pottery Folly
- 1969
Caernarvon castle folly in Keystone pottery, issued to commemorate the investiture of Prince Charles in July 1969.
- *height 21cm*
- £65 • Hope & Glory

Coronation Cup and Saucer
- 1902
Bone china cup and saucer commemorating the coronation of Edward VII. Made by Foley.
- *height 5.5cm*
- £58 • Hope & Glory

Birthday Mug
- 1991
Bone china mug by Aynsley to commemorate the thirtieth birthday of Princess Diana.
- *height 9.5cm*
- £70 • Hope & Glory

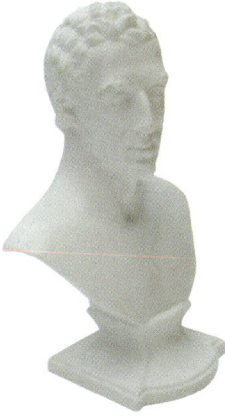

Child's Plate
- 1821
Very unusual child's plate depicting Queen Caroline.
- £325 • Hope & Glory

Bust of Wellington
- circa 1835
Pre-Parian bust of Wellington in Felspar porcelain. Issued by Copeland and Garrett.
- *height 20cm*
- £290 • Hope & Glory

Coins & Medals

Commemorative Coin
- *1935*
A gold coin commemorating the Silver Jubilee of King George V. The coin shows the King and Queen Mary with Windsor Castle on reverse.
- *diameter 31mm*
- £250   • Malcolm Bord

Half-Sovereign Coin
- *1817*
A gold King George III half-sovereign coin.
- *diameter 19mm*
- £250   • Malcolm Bord

Austrian Coin
- *1936*
Gold Austrian 100-schilling coin with Madonna on obverse and Austrian shield on reverse.
- *diameter 32mm*
- £450   • Malcolm Bord

Gold Guinea Coin
- *1794*
A gold George III guinea coin. This issue is known as the "Spadge Guinea".
- *diameter 19mm*
- £200   • Malcolm Bord

Gold Sovereign Coin
- *1553*
Queen Mary fine sovereign coin of thirty shillings. With Queen enthroned and Tudor Rose on reverse. Date in Roman numerals.
- *diameter 44mm*
- £5,000   • Malcolm Bord

George III Crown
- *1750*
A silver George III crown coin, with the early head portrait.
- *diameter 38mm*
- £750   • Malcolm Bord

Silver Penny
- *circa 1025*
A short cross-type silver penny from the court of King Cnut.
- *diameter 32mm*
- £100   • Malcolm Bord

George III Guinea Coin
- *1813*
A gold George III guinea coin. This coin is known as the "Military Guinea".
- *diameter 19mm*
- £800   • Malcolm Bord

Coins & Medals

Russian Medal ▼
- *1915*
Imperial Russian Cross of St. George IV class.
- £45 • Chelsea (OMRS)

Order of the Indian Empire ◄
- *1900*
Order of the Indian Empire Cie breast badge in case of award.
- £450 • Chelsea (OMRS)

Great War Medal ▲
- *1911–37*
A distinguished service order (George V) in Garrard & Co, in case of award.
- £450 • Chelsea (OMRS)

Miniature Medals ▼
- *1918*
A set of KCMG, CB (Gold) group of ten miniatures attributed to Major General Sir Andrew Mitchell Stuart. Royal Engineers.
- £385 • Chelsea (OMRS)

Cap Badge ▲
- *1914–18*
Royal Sussex Regiment silver and enamel officer's cap badge.
- £100 • Chelsea (OMRS)

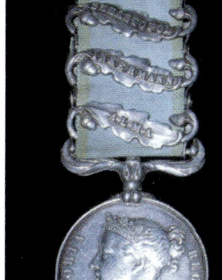

Crimea War Medal ▲
- *1854–56*
A Crimea war medal from 1854, with three clasps, "Alma" "Inkermann" and "Sebastopol". Awarded to G. Bartlett of the 63rd Regiment.
- £350 • Chelsea (OMRS)

Expert Tips

The value of coins depends on their mint mark, design, date and condition, which is graded from FDC (fleur de coin or mint condition) to F (fair). Always have your collection photographed for insurance purposes, and store the information away from the collection.

Memorial Plaque
- *1914*
Great War memorial plaque dedicated to Ernest George Malyon of the 2nd/16th Battalion London Regiment and inscribed "He died for freedom and honour".
- *diameter 12cm*
- £25   • Chelsea (OMRS)

Air Force Medal
- *1945*
A European Aircrew Star, awarded to a serving member of the Royal Air Force in World War II.
- £105   • Chelsea (OMRS)

Military Clasp
- *1943*
World War II German Navy U-boat Clasp for Bravery. Mid-war zinc example by Peeuhaus.
- £575   • Chelsea (OMRS)

Leopold II Medal
- *1915*
Order of Leopold II 2nd Class neck badge.
- £175   • Chelsea (OMRS)

Waterloo Medal
- *1815*
A Waterloo medal, 1815, awarded to Joseph Porch of the 11th Light Dragoons, wounded in action.
- £1,000   • Chelsea (OMRS)

Cap Badge
- *1939–45*
Royal Armoured Corps WWII plastic cap badge.
- £25   • Chelsea (OMRS)

Military Medal Trio
- *1918*
A trio of World War I medals, including the Victory medal, awarded to Private H. Codd of the East Yorkshire Regiment.
- £35   • Chelsea (OMRS)

Ephemera

Thor
- *January 1970*
The Mighty Thor, no. 172, original price one shilling, from Marvel Comics.
- £10
- Gosh

Famous Crowns Series
- *1938*
Set of 25 cards, by Godfrey Phillips Ltd. Illustration shows an Italian crown.
- £8
- Murray Cards

Strange Tales
- *1967*
Strange Tales no.161 – *Doctor Strange – The Second Doom*. Published by Marvel Comics.
- £15
- Book & Comic Exchange

Titanic Series
- *date 1999*
Set of 25 large-scale cards of the *Titanic*, produced by Rockwell Publishing at the time of James Cameron's film.
- £10
- Murray Cards

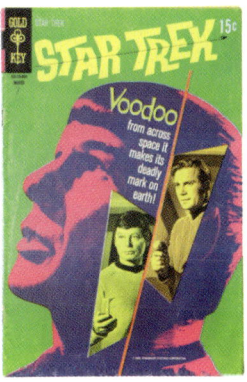

Star Trek
- *1970*
Star Trek no.7 March 1970. Published by Gold Key.
- £50
- Book & Comic Exchange

Superman Series
- *1968*
Set of cards, issued as series 950 by Primrose Confectionery Co, with sweet cigarettes. Illustration shows "Space Nightmare".
- £15
- Murray Cards

Kensitas Flower Series
- *1933*
An unusual series of 60 cigarette collecting items with silk flowers enclosed in envelopes. By J Wix & Sons.
- £168
- Murray Cards

Ray Lowry Cartoon
- *1992*
An original cartoon drawing by Ray Lowry.
- £65
- Gosh

Amazing Spiderman
- February 1966

Amazing Spiderman no. 333 – *The Final Chapter!* – published by Marvel Comics.
- £50 ● Gosh

Searle Lithograph
- circa 1960

A Ronald Searle lithograph from "Those Magnificent Men in Their Flying Machines".
- £420 ● Gosh

Romantic Story
- September 1958

No. 40 – *Love's Tender Moments* – published by Charlton.
- £17.50 ● Gosh

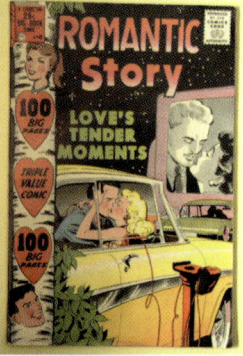

Opera Series
- 1895

Set of six opera cards, collected with products of The Liebig Extract Meat Co, France.
- £80 ● Murray Cards

The Incredible Hulk
- September 1968

The Incredible Hulk, issue no. 107, by Marvel Comics.
- £13.50 ● Gosh

Billiard Series
- circa 1905

Set of 15 cards of *double entendre* billiard terms, from Salmon & Gluckstein.
- £825 ● Murray Cards

Monte Hale
- 1952

Monte Hale Western comic. Issue no. 76, price 10 cents.
- £15
- Book & Comic Exchange

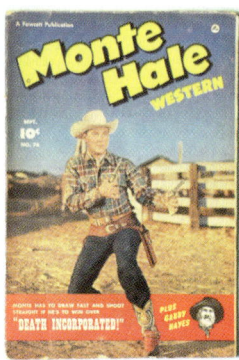

Fantastic Four
- March 1966

Issue no. 48 – *The X-Men!* – published by Marvel Comics.
- £225 ● Gosh

Political Cartoon
- 1997

A political cartoon – *Springs in Spring* – by John Springs.
- £150 ● Gosh

Ephemera

Stan Eales Cartoon ▲
- 1998

A cartoon by Stan Eales of a man standing on the ledge of a burning building.
- £250   • Cartoon Gallery

Blakes 7 ▲
- October 1981

Blakes 7 magazine issue no. 1, published by Marvel UK.
- £8–12
- Book & Comic Exchange

The Dandy ▼
- April 1973

The Dandy, issue no. 1640, published by D.C. Thompson.
- £1   • Gosh

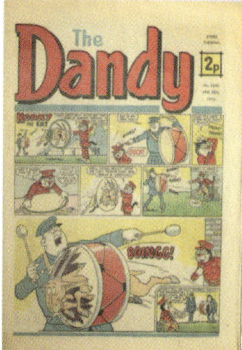

Strange Tales ▼
- March 1964

Strange Tales issue no. 118 – The Human Torch – published by Marvel Comics.
- £17   • Gosh

Playboy ◀
- May 1969

May 1969 issue of *Playboy* magazine, in good condition.
- £6   • Radio Days

Expert Tips

Most magazines launched run to only one issue, so that factor is no rarity. Condition must be excellent.

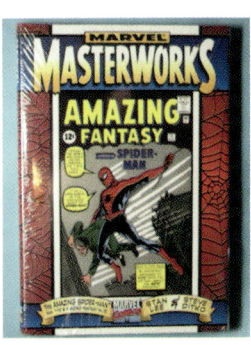

Marvel Masterworks ▲
- 1997

Spiderman volume 1.
- £25   • Gosh

Cricket Series ▲
- circa 1896

Wills's first set of 50 cricketing cigarette cards. Illustration shows Dr W. G. Grace of Gloucestershire.
- £3,250   • Murray Cards

Soho International ▲
- 1971

Volume 1, No. 1.
- £10
- Book & Comic Exchange

National Costumes Series
- 1895
Wills's cigarette cards set of 25. This card shows a Venetian beauty.
- £4,125
- Murray Cards

Famous Film Scene Series
- 1935
Set of 48 cigarette cards, by Gallaher Ltd. Shows Laurel & Hardy from "Babes in Toyland."
- £36
- Murray Cards

Radio Times Cartoon
- 1998
A topical cartoon for *Radio Times* by Kipper Williams.
- £120
- Cartoon Gallery

X-Men
- January 1969
X-Men magazine, issue no. 52 – *Armageddon Now!* – published by Marvel Comics.
- £20
- Gosh

Watchmen
- 1987
The collected edition of a comic original in 12 issues, retelling the super-hero story.
- £14.95
- Gosh

Mayfair Magazine
- 1970
Volume 3, no.1. British edition.
- £20
- Book & Comic Exchange

The Observer Cartoon
- 1997
Political cartoon by Chris Riddell, from *The Observer*.
- £225
- Cartoon Gallery

Expert Tips

A good rule when starting to collect comics is to stick to a particular company, character or artist and collect everything to do with them before moving on.

Buffy the Vampire Slayer
- 1999
Mail order only. Premium Darkhorse publication.
- £10
- Book & Comic Exchange

Ephemera

Vogue
- **November 1946**
A November 1946 copy of *Vogue* by Condé Nast.
- £10
- Radio Days

Builders of the British Empire Series
- **circa 1929**
Set of 50 cards by J A Pattreiouex. Illustration shows General Gordon.
- £135
- Murray Cards

Studio International Art
- **April 1964**
Issue of the art magazine.
- £6
- Book & Comic Exchange

Film Fun
- **1957**
Issue no. 1971. Published by The Amalgamated Press.
- £1.50
- Gosh

Famous Monsters No. 46
- **1967**
Famous Monsters of Filmland.
- £5–10
- Book & Comic Exchange

Witchblade
- **November 1996**
Issue no. 10. Published by Top Cow and signed by the artist.
- £20
- Book & Comic Exchange

Expert Tips

Cigarette cards were mostly made in the USA and English-speaking countries and peaked in the 1930s. Production stopped during the Second World War.

Beatles Series
- **circa 1998**
A set of 10 cards in a limited edition of 2,000. The illustration shows Paul McCartney.
- £5
- Murray Cards

Batman in the Sixties
- **1997**
T.V. series spin-off magazine, published by DC Comics.
- £15
- Gosh

47

Ephemera

Aircraft of the Royal Air Force
- 1938

Set of 50 cigarette cards from Players. Illustration shows Hawker Hurricane.
- £45
- Murray Cards

Sunday Times Cartoon
- 1997

A cartoon for *The Sunday Times* by Nick Newman.
- £120
- Cartoon Gallery

Roses Series
- 1912

Set of 50 cigarette cards from Wills. Illustration shows a Mrs Cocker Rose.
- £50
- Murray Cards

Akira Comic
- 1988

Akira issue no. 2, by Epic publishers. Signed by the translator Frank Yonco.
- £10
- Book & Comic Exchange

Boys' Ranch
- June 1951

Boys' Ranch issue no. 5 – *Great Pony Express Issue* – published by Home Comics.
- £45
- Gosh

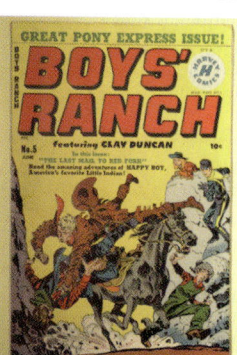

Noted Cats Series
- 1930

Set of 24 cards by Cowans Confectionery, Canada. Shows a Persian male cat.
- £132
- Murray Cards

Notable MPs
- 1929

Series of 50 cigarette cards of politicians, from Carreras Ltd. Illustration shows caricature of David Lloyd George.
- £45
- Murray Cards

Custard Drawing
- 1999

A drawing of the character Custard, by Bob Godfrey, taken from the TV series "Roobarb".
- £130
- Cartoon Gallery

Children of Nations Series
- circa 1900

Set of 12 cards by Huntley & Palmer biscuit manufacturers, for sale in France.
- £66
- Murray Cards

Ephemera

Konga
- 1960
An issue of *Konga* magazine, published by Charlton Comics.
- £15 • Gosh

Incredible Hulk
- 1969
Incredible Hulk, issue no. 112 – *The Brute Battles On!* – published by Marvel Comics.
- £12
- Book & Comic Exchange

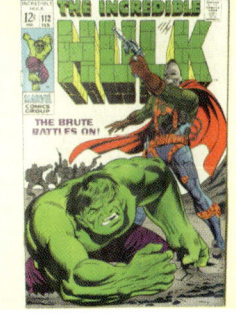

Types of Horses
- 1939
Set of 25 large cigarette cards from John Player & Sons. Illustration shows a Cob horse.
- £85 • Murray Cards

Waterloo Series
- circa 1914
Set of 50 cigarette cards from Wills, never issued from fear of offending the French during First World War.
- £4,750 • Murray Cards

Expert Tips

The French have been producing collectable cards – on products other than cigarettes – since the mid-19th century. Their point-of-sale power was unassailable.

Daredevil
- June 1964
Daredevil issue no. 2, published by Marvel Comics.
- £135 • Gosh

Batman
- May 1942
Very early *Batman* magazine – issue no. 10, by DC Comics.
- £220 • Gosh

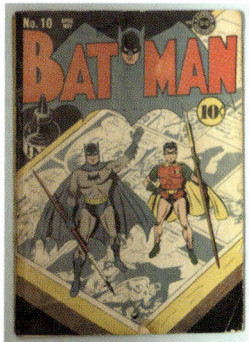

Land Rover Series
- 2000
Set of seven cards, showing seven seater. Illustration shows 86-inch seven-seater.
- £3 • Murray Cards

Magical World of Disney
- circa 1989
Set of 25 cards, from Brooke Bond tea. Illustration shows Mickey Mouse.
- £5 • Murray Cards

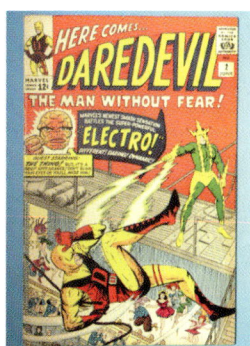

Ephemera

Robotech
- 1985

The *Macross Saga* 7 issue, signed by the translator Frank Yonco with characteristic beard and glasses doodle. Published by Comico comics.
- £8
- Book & Comic

Mad Monsters
- 1964

Issue No. 7 of comic *Mad Monsters*.
- *height 30 cm*
- £1.50
- Book & Comic

Zig Zag
- 1976

Issue No. 65 of rock music magazine *Zig Zag*, with feature on the Beach Boys.
- £4
- Book & Comic

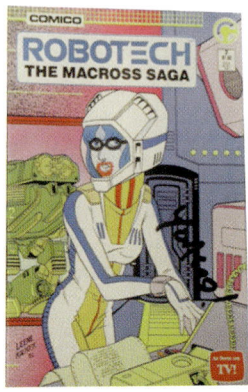

The Beano
- 1969

Issue No. 1,405 of popular UK children's comic, *The Beano*.
- £1
- Book & Comic

The Dr Who Annual
- 1979

1979 annual based on the cult TV series *Dr Who*.
- £5
- Book & Comic

Continental Film Review
- August 1968

August 1968 issue of adult film magazine.
- £3
- Book & Comic

Ephemera

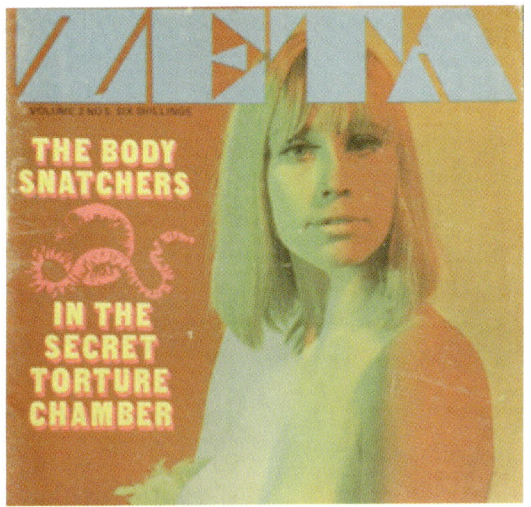

Bomp!
- 1976–77

Music magazine *Bomp!*, featuring Brian Wilson.
- £5   • Book & Comic

Zeta
- 1960s

Issue No. 5, Volume 2, of erotic photography magazine *Zeta*.
- £10   • Book & Comic

Rolling Stone
- 1970

October 1970 issue of US rock music magazine *Rolling Stone*, featuring the life story of Janis Joplin.
- £6   • Book & Comic

Costume Prints
- 1585

A pair of prints by Nicolo Nicolai, depicting courtly figures in Ottoman costumes, displayed in handcrafted frames.
- 39cm x 29cm
- £800   • Chelsea Gallery

Crawdaddy
- July 1973

US music magazine *Crawdaddy*, featuring Marvin Gaye.
- £4   • Book & Comic

Gent
- 1961

Men's magazine *Gent*, featuring interviews with Mark Russell and Klaus Rock.
- £8   • Book & Comic

51

Ephemera

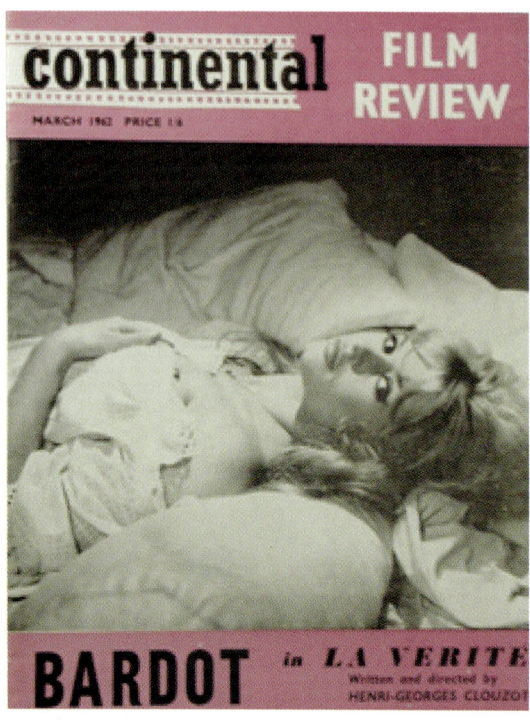

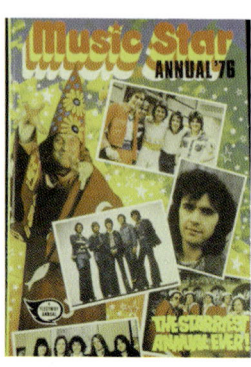

Continental Film Review
- *March 1962*
- March 1962 issue of *Continental Film Review*, featuring Brigitte Bardot on the cover.
- £4
- Book & Comic

International Times
- *1974*
- Issue No. 2, Volume 2, of UK underground newspaper *International Times*.
- £1.50
- Book & Comic

Music Star
- *1976*
- 1976 annual of teenage pop magazine *Music Star*.
- £4
- Book & Comic

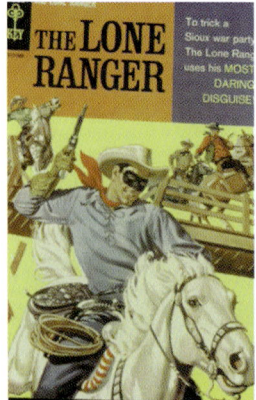

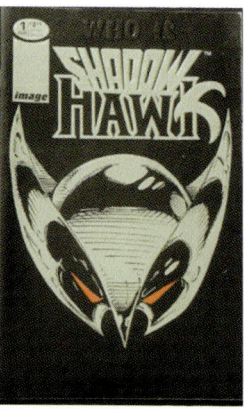

Shadow Hawk
- *1992*
- A first copy of the comic, with a glossy cover.
- *height 30cm*
- £2
- Book & Comic

The Lone Ranger
- *1958*
- *The Lone Ranger* comic book published by Gold Key.
- £6
- Book & Comic

Interview
- *1977*
- Newspaper format of Andy Warhol's magazine, *Interview*.
- £18
- Book & Comic

Kitchenalia

Bell Weight ▼
- circa 1890
A Victorian, two pound, solid brass kitchen weight in very good condition.
- height 11cm
- £22 • Magpies

Pie Funnel ▲
- circa 1890
Roe's patent "Rosebud" ceramic pie funnel, with name on obverse and baking instructions on reverse.
- height 8cm
- £26 • Magpies

Expert Tips
Items falling under the title "kitchenalia" can be defined as "functional kitchen items that have been replaced by more improved and advanced articles for doing the same job".

Chocolate Jug ▼
- circa 1946
Cadbury's salt glaze chocolate jug, hand-painted with the Cadbury's name and logo.
- height 15cm
- £22 • Magpies

Glass Cloche ▼
- circa 1860
A French glass cloche from the mid 19th-century.
- diameter 55cm
- £150 • Gabrielle de Giles

Scales ▲
- circa 1940
Berkel cast iron scales with red enamel finish, spirit level and adjustable foot. Weighs up to 2lb. Made in England.
- height 50cm
- £95 • After Noah

Chamber-Stick ▼
- circa 1890
A late Victorian blue enamel chamber candlestick, with no chips to the enamel.
- diameter 14cm
- £12.50 • Magpies

Stone Sink ◄
- circa 1890
A late Victorian stone sink, with brown glaze to the interior and decorative glaze to the exterior.
- length 95cm
- £120 • Curios

Kitchenalia

Copper & Brass Urn
- circa 1820
Copper and brass urn with brass tap and double-ring handle, banding and finial on a brass pedestal foot.
- height 48cm
- £250   • Rosemary Conquest

> **Expert Tips**
>
> In order to retain their value, it is important that items of kitchenalia should not be purely decorative. They must be complete and in working order.

Herb Chopper
- circa 1880
A Victorian double-handled herb chopping knife.
- length 24cm
- £15   • Magpies

Fish Kettle
- circa 1900
French copper fish kettle of three interlocking pieces.
- length 53cm
- £150   • Youlls

Cordial Syphon
- circa 1934
Fluted, etched glass cordial syphon with brass top.
- height 30cm
- £20   • Magpies

Knife Sharpener
- circa 1890
A Victorian patent knife sharpener with a cast-iron frame.
- height 34cm
- £475   • Drummonds

Salt Tin
- circa 1930
White enamel tin for salt, with black lettering and detailing and domed lid.
- height 26cm
- £18   • Magpies

Flat Iron
- circa 1890
Victorian cast-iron flat iron for use with cooking range.
- length 13cm
- £14   • Magpies

Kitchenalia

Butcher's Block
- *circa 1860*
A 19th-century butcher's block and table with fluted pillars to the front and two cupboards.
- *height 84cm*
- £1,625
- Drummonds

Butcher's Block
- *circa 1910*
Well worn English butcher's block with steel mounts.
- *height 75cm*
- £170
- Myriad

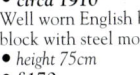

Watering Can
- *circa 1880*
Decorative brass watering can with lattice design, hinged lid and two handles.
- *height 27cm*
- £45
- Magpies

Toaster
- *circa 1930*
A manually-operated toaster made of chrome and painted metal, with bakelite knobs.
- *height 20cm*
- £55
- H. Hay

Teapot
- *circa 1930*
Dartmouth Pottery teapot, with small white dots on a blue ground.
- *height 17cm*
- £38
- Magpies

Copper Funnel
- *circa 1900*
A Victorian copper funnel with removable sieve.
- *height 12cm*
- £18
- Magpies

Steel Footman
- *circa 1800*
Steel footman, for cooking, with cabriole legs on spade feet.
- *height 30cm*
- £200
- Albany

55

Kitchenalia

Novelty Egg Cups
- *circa* 1930s

A group of novelty egg cups, showing cockerel, duck, owl and elephant.
- from £9
- Magpies

Teapot
- *circa* 1932

A "Domino" teapot by T. G. Green, decorated with white dots on a blue ground.
- height 12cm
- £55
- Magpies

Marmalade Jar
- *circa* 1900

A late Victorian, two-tone stoneware jar for storing marmalade or preserves. Originally with cork stopper.
- height 21cm
- £11
- Magpies

Mortar & Pestle
- *circa* 1900

A mortar and pestle, by Mason's, with turned wooden pestle and white ceramic mortar with crest. For grinding spices.
- height 10cm
- £35
- Magpies

Biscuit Barrel
- *circa* 1930s

A novelty Crown Derby biscuit barrel, in the shape of a dog, with black and white detailing, a red nose, brown collar and eyes and a yellow hat doubling as a top.
- height 24cm
- £185
- Beverley

Watering Can
- *circa* 1860

19th-century brass watering can with banding and hinged flap.
- height 39cm
- £115
- Castlegate

Expert Tips

Much kitchenalia is to be found in boot fairs, jumble sales or junk shops. The advantage of junk shops is that they will probably have bought up the entire contents of a house for an agreed price and with the intention of acquiring one or two good items – anything that the vast range of other items fetches is "found" money for them and good value for you.

Bread Knife
- *circa* 1900

A late Victorian bread knife with a stainless steel, serrated blade and a fruitwood handle carved with the word "Bread".
- length 31cm
- £12
- Magpies

Kitchenalia

Scales ▶
- *circa 1940*
Berkel cast iron scales with red enamel finish and spirit level. Weighs up to 2lbs. Made in London.
- *length 50cm*
- £95   • After Noah

Chamber Stick ▲
- *circa 1910*
An Edwardian, enamelled chamber candlestick with floral decoration on a white ground with black, enamel rim.
- *diameter 14cm*
- £14.50   • Magpies

> **Expert Tips**
> *Genuine, practical kitchen and scullery implements tend to be very plain and unfussy. Too much decoration may indicate a later copy.*

Cocoa Tin ▼
- *circa 1890*
A Dutch cocoa tin, inscribed "Cacao C.J. Van Houten & Zoon. Weesp (Holland)", with profusely decorated panels.
- *height 31cm*
- £110   • Rosemary Conquest

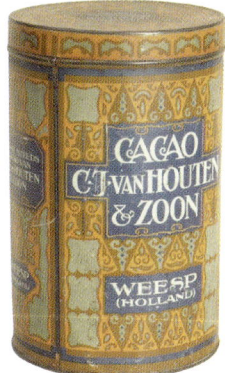

Water Jug ◀
- *circa 1880*
Copper water jug with large splayed lip and tubular handle.
- *height 30cm*
- £46   • Magpies

Rectangular Bread Bin ▼
- *circa 1930*
A rectangular bread bin, enamelled in white, with black lettering and detailing and blue enamelled handles.
- *height 30cm*
- £34   • Magpies

Copper Kettle ▼
- *circa 1870*
A Victorian copper kettle with slender, hooped handle.
- *height 31cm*
- £105   • Castlegate

Fish Kettle ◀
- *circa 1880*
A large, 19th-century copper fish kettle, with rounded ends and two handles.
- *height 19cm*
- £135   • Castlegate

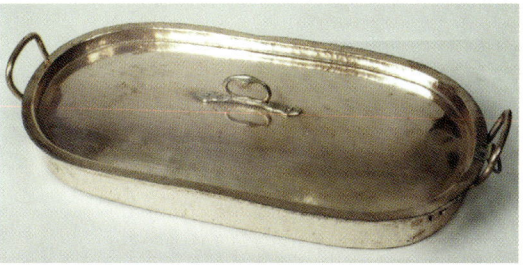

Kitchenalia

Butcher's Block
- *circa 1890*
A French bow-fronted butcher's block table with drawers and cupboards below.
- *length 36cm*
- £2,850
- Drummonds

Toaster
- *circa 1959*
Early classic chrome toaster by Morphy Richards. Immaculate condition.
- *height 19cm*
- £58
- H. Hay

Copper Jug
- *circa 1890*
Water jug in hammered copper, with large splayed lip and armorial frieze.
- *height 26cm*
- £33
- Magpies

Flour Tin
- *circa 1920*
White enamel flour tin with black lettering and detailing and black enamel on the two handles.
- *height 28cm*
- £28
- Magpies

Flour Jar
- *circa 1950*
A white ceramic flour jar with red banded decoration around middle and on the finial top and broad red band to base.
- *height 16cm*
- £32
- Magpies

Ovaltine Mug
- *circa 1950*
Mug promoting the bedtime drink Ovaltine. These mugs were produced in association with their long-running radio show.
- *height 11cm*
- £15
- Magpies

Expert Tips

Even if your kitchenalia isn't worth much, it can still be useful. Redundant graters, for instance, with just the insertion of a candle, make excellent patio lights.

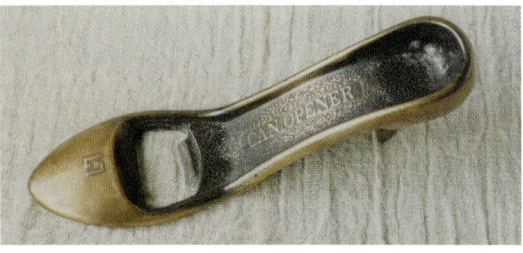

Bottle Opener
- *circa 1920*
A highly collectable Edwardian novelty bottle-opener in the shape of a lady's shoe, made of copper on cast iron.
- *length 12cm*
- £27
- Magpies

Kitchenalia

Potato Cutter
- *1940*
The New "Villa" French fried potato cutter supplied in its original box.
- *26cm x 12cm x 12cm*
- £14
- Radio Days

Mini-Sweeper
- *1940*
Mini-sweeper presented in its original box.
- *20cm x 14cm*
- £12
- Radio Days

Cream Maker
- *1950s*
Bakelite and glass cream maker with alloy handle.
- *height 21cm*
- £15
- Kitchen Bygones

Glass Creamer
- *1940*
Jubilee model glass hand-creamer with primrose yellow plastic cup and handle designed by Bel.
- *height 22cm*
- £16
- After Noah (KR)

Enamelled Bread Bin
- *1940s*
English enamelled bread bin with the letters in stylised font.
- *height 50cm*
- £25
- Kitchen Bygones

Cornish Ware Mug
- *1940*
Cornish ware mug decorated with blue and white hoops.
- *height 8cm*
- £10.50
- Magpies

59

Kitchenalia

Bakelite Thermos
- *1930*

English green Bakelite thermos with metal handle.
- *height 34cm*
- £11
- Magpies

Egg Timer
- *Victorian*

Victorian egg timer with wood-turned column and original glass reservoir.
- *height 14cm*
- £15
- Kitchen Bygones

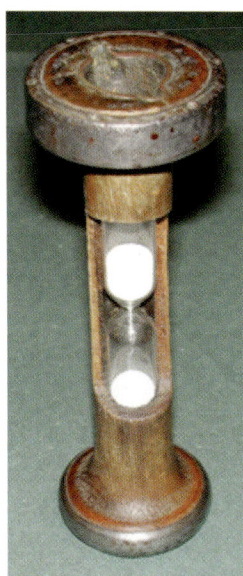

Potato Masher
- *20th century*

Wooden potato masher with turned shaft in fruitwood on a circular wooden base.
- *height 15cm*
- £15
- Kitchen Bygones

Rolling Pin
- *1950s*

Good quality wooden rolling pin with turned painted handles.
- *length 40cm*
- £10
- Kitchen Bygones

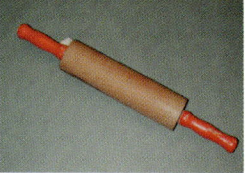

Squeezer
- *1950s*

Solid aluminium vegetable or fruit squeezer made by Atlantic.
- *height 20cm*
- £15
- Kitchen Bygones

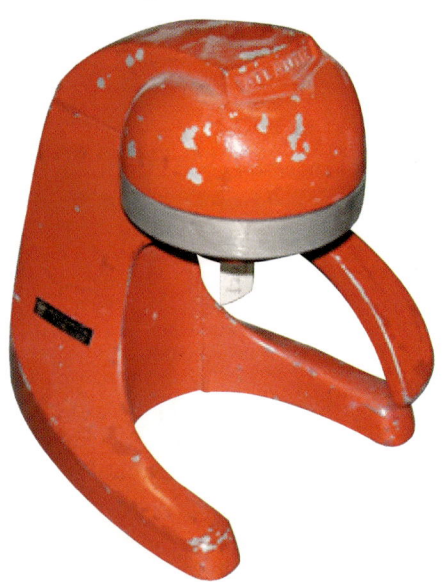

Terracotta Bread Bin
- *20th century*

Terracotta bread bin, with lid and carrying handles.
- *height 33cm*
- £65
- Kitchen Bygones

Kitchenalia

Sugar Sifter
- *circa 1930s*

Sugar sifter by T.G. Green, with blue and white banding.
- *height 28cm*
- £58 • Magpies

Bean Slice
- *1920*

Iron bean slice with a brass handle, produced by Alexander Ware.
- £12 • Magpies

Copper Jelly Moulds
- *circa 1900*

Set of three copper jelly moulds in the shape of oven-ready chickens. Used for making savoury jellies and patés.
- £14 • Magpies

Metal Funnel
- *1940*

Blue enamelled metal funnel with handle.
- *height 17cm*
- £8.50 • Magpies

Ceramic Rolling Pin
- *1950*

Ceramic white rolling pin with green handles, inscribed "Nutbrowne".
- *length 41cm*
- £25 • Magpies

Food Storage Flask
- *1930s*

A vacuum flask for food storage with eagle clasping the world.
- *height 38cm*
- £40 • Kitchen Bygones

Baker's Paddle
- *1920*

A baker's folding paddle with spatulate head.
- *length 185cm*
- £45 • Kitchen Bygones

Kitchenalia

Brass Saucepot ▲
- *1910*

Sauce pot made of brass with iron handles and copper rivets.
- *height 6cm*
- £45   • Magpies

Larder Chest ▲
- *1890*

French Provincial larder chest consisting of four drawers and a cupboard. The whole resting on ogée bracket feet. With original distressed condition.
- *120cm x 90cm*
- £880   • Myriad

Circular Mould ▼
- *1880*

Ring-shaped brass jelly mould.
- *diameter 7cm*
- £24   • Magpies

Hexagonal Mould ▶
- *1890*

Hexagonal-shaped jelly mould in copper.
- *height 11.5cm*
- £11   • Magpies

Shirt-Sleeve Board ▲
- *1920*

Shirt-sleeve ironing board.
- *length 57cm*
- £25   • Kitchen Bygones

Cider Jar ◀
- *1940s*

Stoneware cider jar.
- *height 35cm*
- £25   • Kitchen Bygones

Weighing Scales ◀
- *1940*

Horseshoe-shaped Swedish scales in bronze with enamelled dial and original weighing dish.
- *height 30cm*
- £54   • Magpies

Ink Filler ▲
- *1890*

Copper ink filler fitted with a side handle and a slender copper funnel, used for filling inkwells.
- *height 16cm*
- £35   • Magpies

Expert Tips

It is a marvel how items like these can cast a spell over kitchens, cosy restaurants or bistros. Take care to remember that condition and an attractive patina is the key to success.

Luggage

Leather Trunk
- circa 1910
Small Edwardian trunk of heavy-duty leather with wooden base slats and reinforced corners, sturdy brass catches and locks and two leather restraining straps with fitted loops. Carrying handles are fitted to the middle and to each end. The interior is lined with cotton ticking, compartmentalized and fitted with restraining straps.
- length 79cm
- £70–£150 • Henry Gregory

Crocodile Case
- circa 1928–29
Crocodile case from Garrards of London, made from skin of animal shot by Captain S. J. Bassett in Zanzibar in 1926. With padded satin lining.
- 37cm x 25cm
- £1,500 • Holland & Holland

Expert Tips

Leather luggage to look out for is generally made in London and most reliably by military outfitters. Good luggage is extremely heavy and more for decoration than modern use.

Picnic Hamper
- circa 1940
Made from leather, cane and canvas, with iron fittings and large rope handles at either end.
- length 75cm
- £480 • Myriad Antiques

Victorian Hat Case
- circa 1870
Victorian hat case in hide leather with brass fittings and red quilted interior. Designed to carry two top hats and an opera hat.
- height 87cm
- width 85cm
- £475 • Mia Cartwright

Picnic Case for Two
- circa 1910
English Edwardian leather picnic case, fully fitted with custom-made accoutrements, including chrome-finished hip flask, food storage containers, original Thermos flask, complete bone-handled set of stainless steel cutlery and china crockery.
- width 28cm
- £550 • Mia Cartwright

Suitcases
- 1910
Classic English leather suitcases with brass catches and locks and leather carrying-handles and lined interiors.
- £70 & £150
- Henry Gregory

Hat Box
- circa 1920
Luxury leather hat box, holding several hats, with canvas lining and original travel sticker and initials "K.C." to front. Made in Northampton.
- width 83cm
- £375 • Matthews

Hat Box
- *circa 1870*

Victorian leather hat box with brass fittings and leather handle.
- *35cm x 28cm x 30cm*
- £245
- Henry Gregory

Collar Box
- *circa 1900*

Leather collar box in the shape of a horseshoe.
- *18cm x 17cm x 8cm*
- £48
- Henry Gregory

Top Hat and Box
- *circa 1850*

English leather box for a top hat, with brass fittings and leather strap, with red velvet lining. Complete with hat.
- *38cm x 22cm 35cm*
- £290
- Henry Gregory

Gun Case
- *circa 1900*

English leather gun case with brass fittings and leather handle, having leather straps with brass buckle.
- *84cm x 23cm x 9cm*
- £490
- Henry Gregory

Expert Tips

Old luggage carries an air of sophistication and hints at a decadent past.

Travelling Trunk
- *1850*

English leather brass-studded and bound travelling trunk.
- *42cm x 91cm x 46cm*
- £400
- Tredantiques

Mail Bag
- *circa 1900*

Country house leather mail case with brass fixtures,
- *30cm x 25cm*
- £120
- Henry Gregory

Leather Gladstone Travelling Bag
- *circa 1870*

All-leather Gladstone bag with brass attachments, two straps and double handles.
- *length 69cm*
- £480
- Henry Gregory

Mechanical Music

Polyphon Table Model Style 45
- *circa* 1900

Two-comb, Polyphon Sublime Harmony Piccolo, in superb carved walnut case with floral marquetry. With ten discs.
- £4,950
- Keith Harding

Miniature Musical Box
- *circa* 1890

Two-air music box with the rare tunecard of AMI RIVENC. In fruitwood case inlaid with parquetry. Geneva.
- £750
- Keith Harding

Portable Gramophone
- *circa* 1920

A Japanese portable gramophone, by Mikkephone, with unusual flattened horn speaker and carrying-case with strap.
- *width 30cm*
- £200
- TalkMach

Musical Ballerina
- *circa* 1890

Automaton ballerina, rotating and dancing arabesques. On red plush base. By Rouillet et Decamps.
- £4,500
- Keith Harding

Swiss Musical Box
- *circa* 1850

Swiss musical box of eight tunes. Inlaid with song bird and foliage decoration.
- £3,250
- Pendulum

Cylinder Piano
- *circa* 1860

Small upright domestic piano. Rosewood case with red-cloth frontal, by Hicks of London and Bristol. With 10 tunes.
- £3,300
- Keith Harding

Twelve-Air Musical Box
- *circa* 1890

Exceptionally good Nicole Frères 12-air, two-per-turn, forte-piano musical box, serial number 46094. Outstandingly beautiful case with exquisite marquetry on lid and front. Excellent tone and good musical arrangements of a popular operatic and light classical programme.
- £5,500
- Keith Harding

Musical Box
- circa 1865

Forte Piano by Nicole Frères of Geneva, with eight operatic airs.
- £4,995   • Keith Harding

Art Nouveau Polyphon
- circa 1900

A rare autochange polyphon, from Leipzig, Germany, with 16 22-inch discs and orchestral bells in an Art Nouveau, mahogany case.
- £9,500   • Keith Harding

Phonograph
- circa 1900

An English "Puck" phonograph with large speaker.
- height 35cm
- £250   • TalkMach

Musical Decanter
- circa 1835

A very rare musical decanter of Prussian shape, with a Swiss movement. Plays two tunes.
- £1,250   • Jasmin Cameron

Lecoultre Musical Box
- circa 1890

Musical box in a rosewood case, with original key. Plays six dance tunes, listed on original card.
- £2,400   • Keith Harding

Chiming Table Clock
- circa 1875

Large chiming clock, in fruitwood with gilt brass mounts. Plays Westminster chimes on gongs, Whittington on bells.
- £3,500   • Keith Harding

Musical Box
- circa 1895

Nicole Frères key-wind musical box, playing eight Scottish airs. Rosewood lid with good marquetry in wood and enamel.
- £3,950   • Keith Harding

Mechanical Music

English Organette
- *circa 1910*

By J. M. Draper, England. Fourteen notes, with three stops, flute, expression and principal which operate flaps over the reed box to control the tone.
- £950   • Keith Harding

Phonograph Cylinders
- *circa 1900*

Three phonograph cylinders, two from Edison and one from Bell, in their original packaging.
- £25–45   • TalkMach

Concert Roller Organ
- *circa 1900*

Twenty-key organette by Autophone Company, N.Y. Played by "cobs" or barrels. Ten cobs supplied.
- £1,750   • Keith Harding

Faventia Spanish Street Piano
- *circa 1900*

Two barrels, each playing six tunes. With red-grained finish, on original green and yellow cart.
- £1,495   • Keith Harding

Polyphon Table Model
- *circa 1890*

Rare, style 48, with two combs. Sublime Harmony accompanied by Twelve Saucer Bells. Supplied with eight discs in a walnut case.
- £5,800   • Keith Harding

English Gramophone
- *circa 1915*

An English gramophone by HMV, "His Master's Voice Junior Monarch".
- *height 36cm*
- £3,500   • Keith Harding

> ### Expert Tips
> The Edison Gem and Edison Standard phonographs were produced in vast quantities. Condition needs to be very good to excite the collector.

Dog Model Gramophone
- *circa 1900*

By the Gramophone and Typewriter company. Model number 3. With original brass horn and concert soundbox. Completely overhauled.
- £1,950   • Keith Harding

Miscellaneous

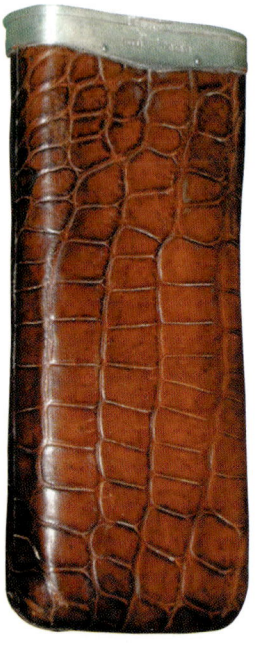

Victorian Cigar Case
- *circa 1900*
A Victorian crocodile skin cigar case with silver trim.
- length 15cm
- £495   • The Reel Thing

Royal Doulton Mug
- *20th century*
A Royal Doulton mug naturalistically moulded as an R.A.F. pilot from World War II.
- height 15cm
- £65   • London Antique

Harlequin Glass Cocktail Set
- *1950*
Harlequin glass cocktail set with brass holder, plastic feet and roped handle.
- 18cm x 35cm
- £25   • Radio Days

Expert Tips
Rubber items will remain well preserved if sprinkled with French chalk.

American Handbag
- *1940*
An American fabric and bamboo handbag with scrolled design.
- 24cm x 28cm
- £150   • Linda Bee

Card Case
- *1870*
Attractive, small crocodile skin card case.
- £125   • The Reel Thing

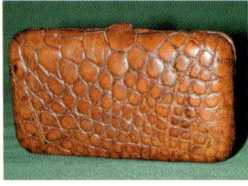

Tortoiseshell Letter Opener
- *1911*
Tortoiseshell letter opener with coins inserted.
- length 20.5cm
- £85   • Abacus Antiques

Miscellaneous

Tortoiseshell Comb
- 1880
Large tortoiseshell comb for hair.
- *height 16cm*
- £95
- Abacus Antiques

Edwardian Shop Scales
- *March 15th, 1906*
Early twentieth-century shop scales inscribed "London & Manchester". Made by the Automatic Scale Company of London & Manchester.
- *33cm x 60cm*
- £125
- Drummonds

Edla Fan and Humidifier
- 1930s
A French Art Deco bakelite fan and humidifier, with a central circular metal cover.
- *height 35cm*
- £200
- Decodence

Alligator Skin Bag
- 1920
An English stitched alligator skin bag with leather handles.
- *55cm x 37cm*
- £175
- John Clay

Hair Grip
- *circa 1900*
Early twentieth century tortoiseshell hair grip.
- *height 13cm*
- £65
- Abacus Antiques

Eye Glass
- 1920
Tortoiseshell eye glass.
- *height 13cm*
- £25
- Abacus Antiques

English Crocodile Skin Bag
- 1920
An English stitched, deep grained, box-shaped, brown crocodile bag with a monogrammed top.
- *42cm x 60cm*
- £150
- John Clay

Miscellaneous

Propeller Clock
- *circa 1917–18*
An Hispana Suiza working clock mounted on a mahogany propeller from a Sopworth Dolphin Scout airplane.
- *260cm x 26cm x 17cm*
- **£1,780**   • Henry Gregory

Bakelite Comb
- *1920*
A French Art Deco bakelite hair comb.
- *length 14cm*
- **£55**   • Linda Bee

Milk Churn
- *1890*
A galvanised steel milk churn of unusual shape with floral garland and swag decoration.
- *height 65cm*
- **£380**   • Myriad

Card Case
- *1880*
A pink mother-of-pearl card case decorated with birds.
- *height 9cm*
- **£155**   • Japanese Gallery

Perpetual Calendar
- *20th century*
An early twentieth century English perpetual calendar.
- **£85**   • North West 8

Barrel Decanter
- *1880*
Walnut barrel decanter.
- *20cm x 6cm*
- **£825**   • Langfords Marine

Miscellaneous

Beehive
- **1890**

A most unusual English beehive, with original basket work with wooden finial.
- *height 70cm*
- **£120**
- Myriad

Crocodile Handbag
- **1940**

A 1940s classically elegant Argentinian crocodile skin handbag with brass trim.
- *23cm x 28cm*
- **£195**
- Linda Bee

American Handbag
- **1960**

An American handbag made from black velvet with gold metal geometric bands and shiny black perspex handle and lid.
- *20cm x 17cm*
- **£150**
- Linda Bee

Pack of Cigarettes
- **1940**

Original 1940s cigarettes branded "Dandy, Special Virginia".
- **£20**
- Linda Bee

Poodle Handbag
- **1950**

A fun American handbag in laminated fabric with poodles on the front.
- *19cm x 28cm*
- **£125**
- Linda Bee

World War I Truncheon
- *circa 1915*

World War I reserve truncheon with leather strap.
- *38cm x 4cm*
- **£160**
- Henry Gregory

Lizard Skin Handbag
- **1950**

A 1950s classic black lizard skin bag.
- *24cm x 37cm*
- **£95**
- Linda Bee

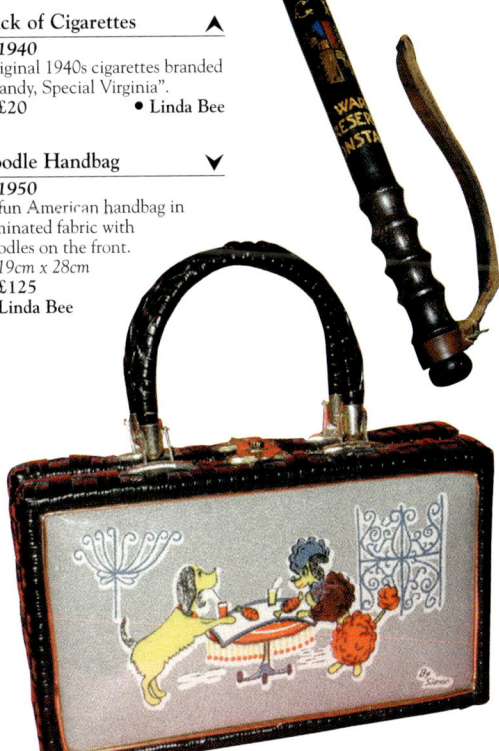

Paperweights

American "Cherries"
- *late 19th century*
American glass paperweight with central cherry pattern on a white latticino ground.
- diameter 7cm
- £620
- G.D. Coleman

Expert Tips

The most collectable of glass paperweights were made between 1845 and 1849 at the French factories in Clichy, Baccarat and St Louis – all well represented here.

Clichy Blue Swirl
- 1848
A rare Clichy swirl glass paperweight in blue and white with central pink and white cones.
- diameter 7cm
- £1,350
- G.D. Coleman

St Louis Paperweight
- *circa 1855*
A St Louis glass paperweight with a mauve, dahlia flower pattern with green leaves.
- diameter 8cm
- £1,350
- G.D. Coleman

Paul Ysart Paperweight
- *circa 20th century*
Quality paperweight by Paul Ysart with a PY signature cane.
- diameter 8cm
- £480
- G.D. Coleman

Baccarat Blue Primose
- *circa 1850*
Baccarat glass paperweight showing a blue primrose and leaves on a clear ground with star cut base. Good condition.
- diameter 5.5cm
- £1,250
- G.D. Coleman

Baccarat Scrambled
- *circa 1850*
Paperweight of a type called "End of Day", since they were made after hours by glass workers with leftovers from the floor.
- diameter 8cm
- £580
- G.D. Coleman

Green Jasper
- *circa 1860*
Mid-19th-century St Louis paperweight with flowers on a green jasper ground.
- diameter 6cm
- £380
- G.D. Coleman

Paperweights

Baccarat Pansy
- *circa 1850*
French Baccarat paperweight, inset with a red pansy and green foliage, on stonecut base.
- *diameter 5.5cm*
- £680   • G.D. Coleman

Floral St Louis ▲
- 1850
St Louis paperweight with pink floral cone design.
- *diameter 6.5cm*
- £7,850   • G.D. Coleman

Sturbridge ▼
- *circa 1880*
English Sturbridge Victorian concentric paperweight with multi-coloured cane design.
- *diameter 8cm*
- £380   • G.D. Coleman

Bohemian Magnum ▼
- 1890
Glass hexagonal paperweight with an etched glass coat of arms with amber faceted flank.
- *11.5cm*
- £380   • G.D. Coleman

Baccarat Sulphite ▼
- 1976
Baccarat sulphite paperweight in facetop form, faceted with six lozenge cuts printed with a bust of Queen Elizabeth II.
- *diameter 7cm*
- £1,670   • London Antique

Wedgwood Plaque ▲
- 1977
Glass paperweight with Wedgwood plaque of Queen Elizabeth II.
- *diameter 7cm*
- £150   • London Antique

Faceted Baccarat ▶
- 1976
Baccarat sulphite paperweight in facetop form. Faceted with six lozenge cuts printed with a bust of Prince Charles.
- *diameter 7cm*
- £2,670   • London Antique

Photographs

Coronation Photograph
- 12th May 1937
George VI coronation photograph, by Dorothy Wilding. Autographed by the King and Queen Elizabeth.
- £2,000
- The Armoury

Silver Gelatin Print
- 20th century
Photograph "Andy, Bob & Elvis" by Nat Finkelstein.
- length 11.5cm
- £550
- Photographers' Gallery

Expert Tips

It may seem facile to advise against damp and direct sunlight with regard to vintage photographs, but these are largely the reasons for their scarcity.

French Photograph Album
- circa 1890
Brass-bound album with several plates of photographs.
- length 23cm
- £165
- Castlegate

Colour Fresson Print
- 1996
New York colour Fresson print by Delores Marat.
- length 45cm
- £800
- Photographers' Gallery

Cyanotype Photograph
- 20th century
Plate entitled "Large Anenome" by Sheva Fruitman.
- length 15cm
- £325
- Photographers' Gallery

C-Type Colour Print
- 20th century
Adam Barfos, "Conference Building Elevators", from his International Territory series.
- length 50cm
- £1,000
- Photographers' Gallery

Silver Gelatin Print
- 1951
"Maidens in Waiting, Blackpool". One of a series by Bert Hardy.
- £500
- Photographers' Gallery

Photographs

Signed Gelatin Print
- 1965

"Ringo" by John "Hoppy" Hopkins. Featuring John Lennon.
- length 30cm
- £350
- Photographers' Gallery

Signed C-Type
- 1965

"Hulme" by Shirley Baker.
- length 40cm
- £250
- Photographers' Gallery

C-Type Print
- 20th century

Signed recto by Julian Germain from "Soccer Wonderland" series.
- length 30cm
- £300
- Photographers' Gallery

Colour Landscape
- 20th century

Untitled print from "Moving Landscape" series by Chrystel Lebas. Edition of ten, signed verso.
- £450
- Photographers' Gallery

Signed C-Type
- 1998

Signed limited edition of three, "Lina", by Annelies Strbar.
- length 17.5cm
- £1,320
- Photographers' Gallery

Silver Gelatin Print
- 20th century

"Monsieur Plitt Teaching Tupy to Jump over the Brook" by Jacques-Henri Lartigue.
- length 75cm
- £1,850
- Photographers' Gallery

Signed Gelatin Print
- 1958

"Swimming Pool, Welch, West Virginia" by O. Winston Link.
- length 50cm
- £1,350
- Photographers' Gallery

Photographs

Cibachrome Print
- *20th century*
Untitled from "The Wild West" series by David Levinthal. Edition limited to 25.
- *length 25cm*
- £500
- Photographers' Gallery

Estate Print
- *20th century*
"Asleep on the job" by Weegee. Silver gelatin print.
- *length 27.5cm*
- £500
- Photographers' Gallery

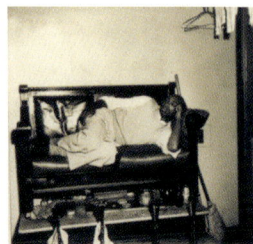

Signed Gelatin Print
- *1953*
"Nude, Eygalieres, France" by Bill Brandt. Signed recto.
- *length 50cm*
- £1,500
- Photographers' Gallery

C-Type Print
- *20th century*
Untitled girl in hammock photograph by Nat Finkelstein.
- *length 30cm*
- £550
- Photographers' Gallery

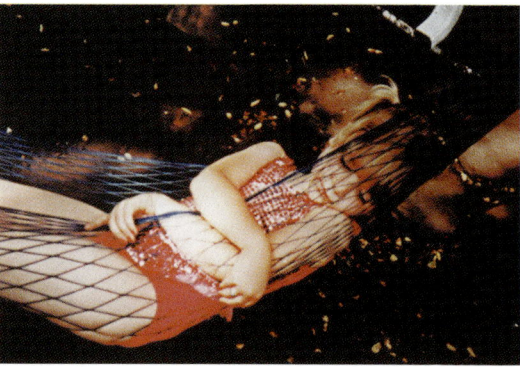

Silver Gelatin Print
- *1957*
"Vali Reflected in the Mirror" by Ed Van der Elsken.
- *length 42cm*
- £650
- Photographers' Gallery

Paris Print
- *1951*
"Claudy and Vali in Claudy's Hotel Room" by Ed Van der Elsken.
- *£2,050*
- Photographers' Gallery

Photograph Album
- *circa 1890*
Brass-mounted book with mother-of-pearl and rosewood inlay.
- *length 23cm*
- £295
- Castlegate

Photographs

Shirley Baker Print ▼
- *1964*
- "Salford, 1964" by Shirley Baker. A silver gelatin print, signed verso.
- 30.5cm x 35.5cm
- £200 • Photo. Gallery

Silver Gelatin Print ▼
- *1955*
- James Dean on the set of *Rebel Without a Cause* by photographer Bob Willoughby. Silver gelatin print, signed verso.
- 30.5cm x 40cm
- £400 • Photo. Gallery

Matthew Murray Print ▼
- *1999*
- "Morris Dancers, 1999" by Matthew Murray. C-Type print, signed verso.
- 30.5cm x 35.5cm
- £200 • Photo. Gallery

Signed Willoughby Print ▶
- *1962*
- "Billie Holliday, Tiffany Club, 1962" by Bob Willoughby. A silver gelatin print, signed verso.
- 30.5cm x 35.5cm
- £400 • Photo. Gallery

Signed C-Type Print ▲
- *1952*
- Marilyn Monroe photographed in 1952 by Bob Willoughby. C-Type print, signed verso.
- 30.5cm x 40cm
- £600 • Photo. Gallery

Lartique Print ▼
- *1931*
- "Cours automobile à Monthery, 1931" by Jacques-Henri Lartique. A silver gelatin print, signed verso.
- 30.5cm x 35.5cm
- £2,800 • Photo. Gallery

Bob Willoughby Print ◀
- *1962*
- "Audrey Hepburn, 1962" by Bob Willoughby. A silver gelatin print, signed verso.
- 25.5cm x 30.5cm
- £600 • Photo. Gallery

Expert Tips

Pictures of famous people, from film stars to politicians, including those who have fallen from fame, often make a good investment. Fewer prints in circulation usually leads to an increase in their value.

Photographs

Silver Gelatin Print
- 1987

"North Islands in dry docks, Smith's Dock 1987" by Ian Macdonald. Silver gelatin print, signed verso.
- 51cm x 35.5cm
- £600   • Photo. Gallery

C-Type Print
- 1999

Untitled C-type print by photographer Nigel Shafran. Signed verso.
- 25.5cm x 35.5cm
- £300   • Photo. Gallery

Untitled Print
- circa 1950

Untitled silver gelatin print from the 1950s, signed recto by photographer Bert Hardy.
- 12cm x 16cm
- £1,300   • Photo. Gallery

Expert Tips

Look out for prints that capture a freak or unusual moment, or that portray a familiar subject in surroundings that are out of context. Some photographs are now ranked alongside art so it is worth concentrating on collecting the work of a favourite up-and-coming photographer.

Signed C-Type Print
- 2000

"Kitchen Sink" by Nigel Shafran. C-type print, signed verso.
- 51cm x 35.5cm
- £750   • Photo. Gallery

Ian Macdonald Print
- circa 1980

Untitled silver gelatin print by photographer Ian Macdonald. Signed verso.
- 30.5cm x 40cm
- £500   • Photo. Gallery

Untitled C-Type Print
- 1998

Untitled C-type print taken in 1998 by Jason Oddy, from the "Palace of Nations" series. Signed verso.
- 30.5cm x 35.5cm
- £500   • Photo. Gallery

Photographs

Silver Gelatin Print
- *1937*

Signed silver gelatin print by Humphrey Spender of two small children playing on a wasteland in Bolton, Lancashire. For mass observation
- *30.5cm x 40cm*
- £300   • Photo. Gallery

Signed Brandt Print
- *1956*

"Nude, London, 1956" by Bill Brandt. A silver gelatin print, signed recto.
- *30.5cm x 40cm*
- £1,800   • Photo. Gallery

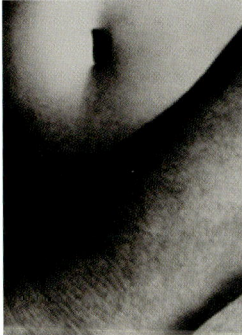

Bill Brandt Print
- *1930*

"Parlour Maid at Window, Kensington, 1930" by Bill Brandt. Silver gelatin print, signed recto.
- *30.5cm x 40cm*
- £1,300   • Photo. Gallery

Limited C-Type Print
- *1965*

"Edie Sedgwick in Red Dress, 1965" by Nat Finkelstein. C-type print, from a limited edition of eight. Signed and numbered verso.
- *30.5cm x 40cm*
- £650   • Photo. Gallery

Limited Edition Print
- *1965*

"Andy and Cow Wallpaper, 1965" by Nat Finkelstein. Silver gelatin print from an edition limited to 10. Signed verso.
- *30.5cm x 40cm*
- £600   • Photo. Gallery

Signed Silver Gelatin
- *circa 1994*

"Milton Keynes" by Leo Regan. Silver gelatin print, signed verso
- *30.5cm x 40cm*
- £300   • Photo. Gallery

Photographs

John Hopkins Print
- 1964

"Thelonius Monk" taken in 1964 by John 'Hoppy' Hopkins. Silver gelatin print, signed recto.
- 30.5cm x 40cm
- £350   • Photo. Gallery

Cornel Lucas Print
- 1948

"Yvonne de Carlo as Salome" by Cornel Lucas. A silver gelatin print, signed recto and titled verso.
- 30.5cm x 40cm
- £400   • Photo. Gallery

Silver Gelatin Print
- 1948

"Movie cameraman in the South Pacific, 1948" by Cornel Lucas. Silver gelatin print, signed recto.
- 30.5cm x 40cm
- £400   • Photo. Gallery

C-Type Print
- 2000

"Hot Dandelion, 2000" by photographer Delilah Dyson. C-type print, signed verso.
- 30.5cm x 40cm
- £250   • Photo. Gallery

Humphrey Spender Print
- 1937

"Bolton, 1937" by Humphrey Spender. For mass observation. Silver gelatin print, signed and titled recto.
- 30.5cm x 40cm
- £300   • Photo. Gallery

Signed Print
- 2000

"Snow Drops, 2000" by Delilah Dyson. C-type print, signed verso.
- 30.5cm x 40cm
- £300   • Photo. Gallery

Silver Gelatin Print
- 1955

"The Popes and the last passenger steam train, 1955" taken by O. Winston Link.
Silver gelatin print, signed verso by the photographer.
- 30.5 x 40cm
- £1,750   • Photo. Gallery

Posters

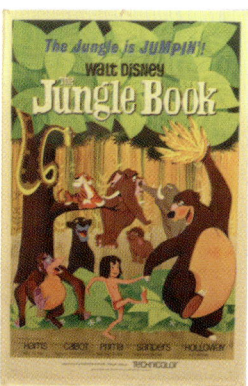

Jungle Book Poster
- circa 1967

Released by Buena Vista with credits to voice talents.
- length 1m, width 69cm
- £300 • Reel Poster Gallery

2001: A Space Odyssey
- circa 1968

Entitled "The Ultimate Trip" and signed by Kaplan.
- length 1m, width 69cm
- £3,000 • Reel Poster Gallery

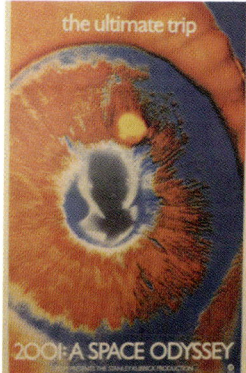

Goldfinger Poster
- circa 1964

Original French poster by Jeism Mascii. Released by United Artists. Captions in French.
- length 79cm, width 61cm
- £500 • Reel Poster Gallery

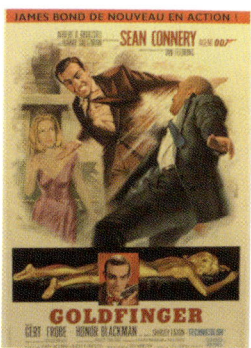

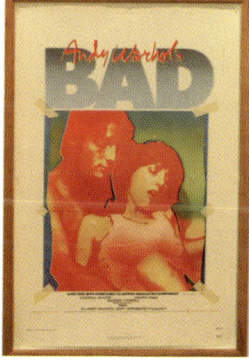

Andy Warhol's "Bad"
- circa 1977

Artwork by John Van Hamersveld. With caption.
- length 1m, width 69cm
- £325 • Reel Poster Gallery

Coca-Cola Card Sign
- circa 1940

A Coca-Cola card sign with caption "Have a Coke".
- height 65cm
- £115 • Dodo

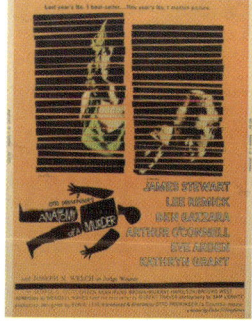

Anatomy of Murder
- circa 1959

Graphic artist style by Saul Bass. Photographs by Sam Leavitt.
- length 1m, width 76cm
- £850 • Reel Poster Gallery

Expert Tips

The quality of a film poster itself is more important than the quality of the film it is promoting, but rarity value plays a big part – hence the high value placed on Belgian versions.

Stand-Up Card Sign
- circa 1940

A Hartley's three-dimensional stand-up card sign.
- height 53cm
- £160 • Dodo

Posters

Card Sign
- *circa* 1900
A Kenyon & Craven's card sign advertising jams and marmalade.
- height 40cm
- £245
- Dodo

Curse of Frankenstein
- *circa* 1957
Japanese, paper-backed and signed by Christopher Lee.
- length 76cm, width 51cm
- £950
- Reel Poster Gallery

Showcard
- *circa* 1950
A showcard advertising Twinsol pure wool socks.
- height 65cm
- £20
- Radio Days

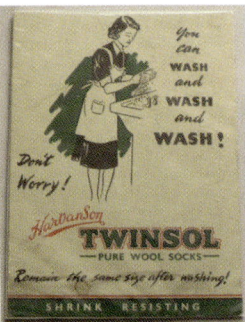

Star Wars Poster
- *circa* 1977
With Polish translation and paper-backed. Artwork by Jakub Enol.
- length 97cm, width 69cm
- £425
- Reel Poster Gallery

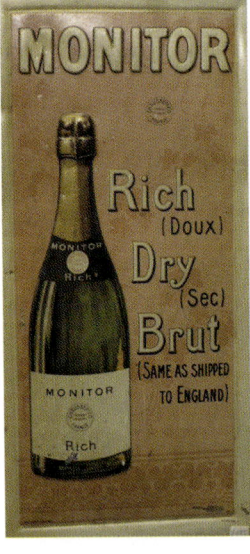

Un Homme et une Femme
- *circa* 1966
A montage of photo images from the film, in Eastman colours.
- length 79cm, width 61cm
- £1,250
- Reel Poster Gallery

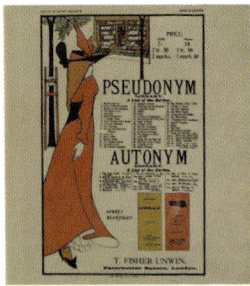

Pseudonym Autonym
- *circa* 1890
An Aubrey Beardsley original poster. English but printed in France.
- length 50cm
- £380
- Victor Arwas

Embossed Tin Sign
- *circa* 1910
An embossed tin sign showing an advertisement for alcohol.
- height 31cm
- £175
- Dodo

Posters

Get Carter
- circa 1971
With photographic captions from the film by M.G.M.
- length 1m, width 69cm
- £425   • Reel Poster Gallery

"Reine de Joie" Poster
- circa 1890
An original poster showing a large man with a lady in a red dress on his lap.
- length 30cm
- £800   • Victor Arnas

Le Mans
- circa 1971
French poster showing Steve McQueen. Artist Rene Fenacci.
- length 61cm, width 41cm
- £150   • Reel Poster Gallery

Jess II Bandito
- circa 1939
Showing actor Tyrone Power. Released by 20th Century Fox.
- length 2m, width 1.4m
- £1,800   • Reel Poster Gallery

Sleeping Beauty
- circa 1959
A paper-backed poster of Walt Disney's *Sleeping Beauty* showing various characters from the story and the title "Awaken to a World of Wonders!".
- length 76cm, width 51cm
- £300   • Reel Poster Gallery

Planet of the Apes
- circa 1968
A linen-backed, cartoon style Romanian poster with title "Planeta Maimutelor".
- length 97cm, width 69cm
- £950   • Reel Poster Gallery

Psycho
- circa 1960
Showing Alfred Hitchcock on a blank background. Printed in England by W. E. Berry and released by Paramount Pictures. In style B.
- length 1m, width 76cm
- £5,000   • Reel Poster Gallery

Posters

Gimme Shelter ▼
- 1970

Original US poster, paper backed, for the Rolling Stones' film *Gimme Shelter*.
- 104cm x 69cm
- £350 • Reel Poster Gallery

Rebellion/Bunt ►
- 1967

Original Polish poster, paper backed, featuring artwork by Rapnicki.
- 84cm x 58cm
- £150 • Reel Poster Gallery

Jour de Fête ◄
- 1948

Original French poster, linen backed, for the Jacques Tati film *Jour de Fête*, featuring artwork by Eric.
- 160cm x 119cm
- £2,500
- Reel Poster Gallery

Przygoda L'Avventura ▲
- 1959

Original Polish poster, paper backed, by Jan Lenica.
- 84cm x 58cm
- £250 • Reel Poster Gallery

Viaggio in Italia ▲
- 1953

Original Italian poster, linen backed, by Mauro Innocenti for the film *Viaggio in Italia*.
- 201cm x 140cm
- £1,800 • Reel Poster Gallery

Que Viva Mexiko ◄
- 1932

Original east German poster, paper backed, by Wenzer.
- 81cm x 58cm
- £180 • Reel Poster Gallery

Posters

F for Fake
- 1973
Original US poster, linen backed, designed by Donn Trethewey.
- *104cm x 69cm*
- £500 • Reel Poster Gallery

The Graduate
- 1967
Original US poster, linen backed, designed by United Artists Corporation.
- *206cm x 104cm*
- £2,250 • Reel Poster Gallery

Turtle Diary
- 1985
Original British poster, paper backed, featuring artwork by Andy Warhol, for the film *Turtle Diary*.
- *76cm x 102cm*
- £225 • Reel Poster Gallery

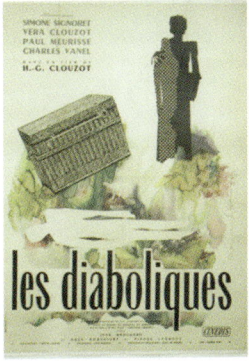

Les Diaboliques
- 1955
Original French poster, linen backed, style A, with artwork by Raymondgid.
- *160cm x 119cm*
- £1,500 • Reel Poster Gallery

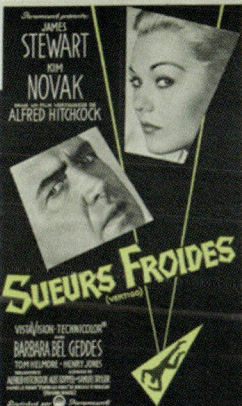

La Donna Che Visse due Volte/Vertigo
- 1958
Original Italian poster featuring art by Sandro Simeoni, for the Hitchcock film *Vertigo*.
- *140cm x 99cm*
- £1500 • Reel Poster Gallery

Expert Tips
The condition and rarity of a poster enhance its value, so focus on these factors. Film posters distributed and printed in small countries have become rare and are a good investment.

Sueurs Froides/Cold Sweat
- 1958
Original French poster, paper backed, art by Claude Venin.
- *79cm x 61cm*
- £425 • Reel Poster Gallery

85

Radio, TV & Sound Equipment

Bendix Model 526C
- 1946

Black Bakelite American radio with the inscription "Strong Machine Age".
- 28cm x 35cm
- £750   • Decodence

Fada Streamliner
- 1940

American onyx and amber streamlined Catalin radio, with large oval dial on the right.
- height 19cm
- £1,000   • Decodence

GEC Radio
- circa 1950

GEC radio with Bakelite handles.
- 32cm x 44cm x 17cm
- £55   • Radio Days

Intercom Speaker
- 1940s

English Art Deco-style red intercom system speaker, tube operated.
- height 28cm
- £100   • Decodence

Sonorette
- 1940s

French brown radio in bakelite, with a bulbous form and grille-design speaker.
- height 34cm
- £500   • Decodence

Emersa Radio
- 1932

American Art Deco Bakelite radio with a central fan design.
- 40cm x 50cm
- £300   • Decodence

Radio, TV & Sound Equipment

Ekco Table Model ▲
- *circa 1939*
Model TA201. Original price 22 guineas. Vision only (sound was obtained by tuning a suitable radio to the TV channel).
- *height 50cm*
- £600 • Vintage Wireless

"KB" Wooden Radio ▲
- *circa 1940*
Fully working radio. One of many produced in Great Britain during the Second World War.
- *height 46cm*
- *width 53cm*
- £125 • Radio Days

Bush TV ▼
- *circa 1949*
22 Model. Most desired of all British Bakelite TVs.
- *height 39cm*
- £300 • Decodence

TV/Radio & Gramophone ▼
- *1938*
R.G.D. (Radio Gramophone Developments) model RG. Top of the range radiogram. Image viewed through mirror in the lid.
- *height 92.5cm*
- £3,250 • Vintage Wireless

CKCO Model AD75 ▲
- *circa 1940*
Wartime English bakelite radio designed by Wells Coates to meet marine needs.
- *height 35cm*
- £700 • Decodence

Expert Tips

The Second World War was the golden age of radio production in the UK. The government needed the medium for morale purposes and insisted on economical manufacture.

Marconi Mastergram ▼
- *1937*
Model 703 TV/radio/auto-radiogram. Same chassis as HMV equivalent and originally costing 120 guineas.
- *height 97.5cm*
- £3,000 • Vintage Wireless

Silver Tone Bullet 6110 ◄
- *circa 1938*
Modern design push-button radio with enormous rotating turning scale. Designed by Clarence Karstacht.
- *height 17cm*
- £1,100 • Decodence

Invicta Table Model
- date 1939
Model TL5, made by Pye of Cambridge. This is the only known model of Invicta.
- height 47.5cm
- £800 • Vintage Wireless

Philips Radio
- circa 1931
Hexagonal with oxidised bronze grill. Sought after for its unusual appearance.
- height 43cm
- £500 • Decodence

Crystal Set
- circa 1910
An English Edwardian crystal set in mahogany case with brass fittings. In good condition.
- height 30cm
- £585 • TalkMach

Grille Radio
- circa 1945
Chunky automobile fender grille radio. Made by Sentinel. Very desirable.
- height 19cm
- £1,000 • Decodence

JVC Television
- circa 1968
A JVC "Space Helmet" television of spherical form on a square plinth. Monochrome reception.
- height 60cm
- £200 • TalkMach

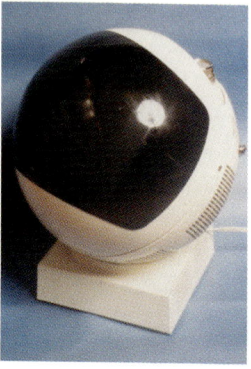

Portable Radio
- circa 1955
A small portable radio with original leather protective case. Medium and long waves.
- height 11cm
- £45 • TalkMach

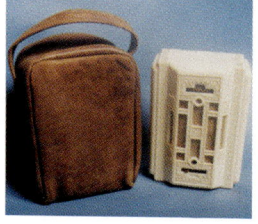

Expert Tips

Most radios need to be in full working order; if they are not, then they need to be remarkably unusual or celebrity-connected to be collectable.

Mains Radio
- circa 1950
A very small, red-cased mains radio by Packard Bell of the U.S.A., with large central dial and minimal controls.
- height 14cm
- £140 • TalkMach

Rock & Pop

Manic Street Preachers Single
- 1990
"UK Channel Boredom" flexi-disc supplied with both fanzines.
- 18cm x 18cm
- £120 • Music & Video

Strawbs with Sandy Denny Album
- 1969
Strawbs music sampler No. 1, issued as a limited edition of 100.
- 30cm x 30cm
- £675 • Music & Video

U2 Helmet
- 1998
U2 helmet issued to promote the *Best of 1980–1990* album. Limited edition of 50 units.
- 30cm x 25cm x 23cm
- £250 • Music & Video

Powder Compact
- circa 1963
Circular powder compact featuring a Dezo Hoffman black and white shot of The Beatles.
- £475 • More Than Music

U2 Single
- 1979
U2's first single "Three", individually numbered.
- 20cm x 30cm
- £350 • Music & Video

Madonna Lucky Star Single
- 1983
Full-length version of the single "Lucky Star" by Madonna.
- 30cm x 30cm
- £80 • Music & Video

Rolling Stones Album
- 1971
Export edition of Rolling Stones *Stone Age* album.
- 30cm x 30cm
- £700 • Music & Video

Rock & Pop

At Home With Screamin' Jay Hawkins
- circa 1958

Album by the late Jay Hawkins – known for the epic single "I Put a Spell on You".
- £499   • Music & Video

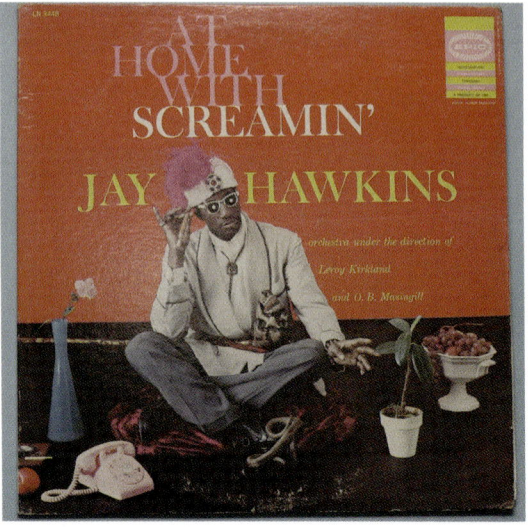

Beatles Parlophone A Label Demo
- 1967

A green A Label demo disc, featuring "Hello Goodbye" and "I am the Walrus".
- £800   • More Than Music

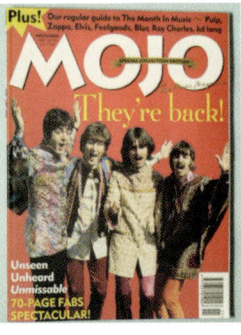

Mojo Magazine
- circa 1995

Issue no. 24 showing The Beatles. Published in three colours – this one with a red background.
- £20
- Book & Comic Exchange

John Lennon Mug
- circa 1987

One of a limited edition of 1,000 Royal Doulton mugs, modelled by Stanley James Taylor.
- £750   • More Than Music

Wings Album
- circa 1979

Back to the Egg promo. Only picture disc manufactured for the MPL Christmas Party 1979.
- £1,350   • Music & Video

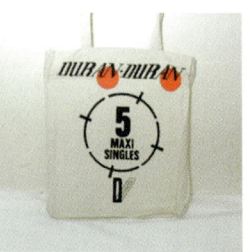

Tote Bag with Five 12-inch Singles
- 1985

Duran Duran tote bag containing five maxi 12-inch singles.
- 30cm x 35cm
- £75   • Music & Video

Rolling Stones Album
- 1975

Japanese five LP, 62-track promo of *The Great History of The Rolling Stones*. Box comes with large book and OBI. Individually printed inner sleeves.
- £347   • Music & Video

Expert Tips

The most desirable objects are personal items belonging to the stars – such as clothes and instruments – preferably accompanied by a photograph of the star using or wearing them.

Rock & Pop

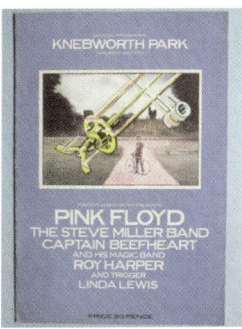

Knebworth Park ▲
- date 5th July 1974

Official programme for Pink Floyd's open-air concert at Knebworth Park.
- £65 • Music & Video

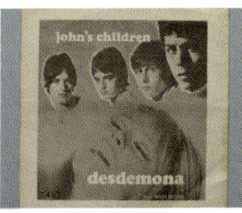

John's Children ▲
- circa 1967

Copy of *Desdemona* by John's Children, featuring Marc Bolam and banned by the BBC.
- £100 • Music & Video

Iron Maiden Picture Disc ▼
- circa 1983

A picture disc of Iron Maiden's *Peace of Mind* album, illustrated on both sides.
- £40 • Music & Video

The Verve ▼
- circa 1992

Mint condition copy of *Voyager 1*, recorded live in New York, by The Verve.
- £65 • Music & Video

Mojo ▲
- circa 1995

Mojo issue no. 24 showing The Beatles. Published with three different covers, this one with a blue background.
- £20
- Book & Comic Exchange

Expert Tips

Brian Epstein, The Beatles' manager, was famously dismissive of the value of merchandising. As a result, "official" souvenirs proliferate and prices are unpredictable.

Beatles Sketch ▼
- circa 1967

An original sketch of Paul McCartney from The Beatles' film *Yellow Submarine*.
- £300 • Music & Video

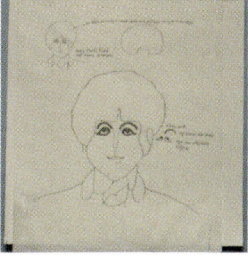

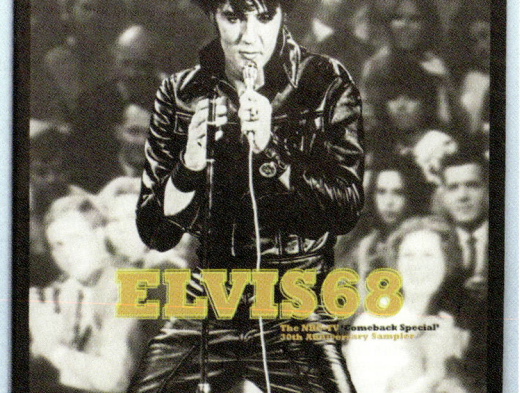

Elvis 68 ◄
- circa 1988

A copy of the NBC TV 'Comeback Special' commemorative Elvis Presley promotional album.
- £125 • Music & Video

Beatles Archive Footage
- 1964

Two four-minute standard 8, silent, black and white reels. Of *London and Kennedy Airports* and *The Beatles Triumphant Appearance in the U.S.A.* In original box.
- £195 each
- More Than Music

Untied Diaries Box Set
- 1988

Untied Diaries edition 30, with 32 cassettes individually recorded and packaged. This is different from the vinyl version.
- £900
- Music & Video

Beatles Dress
- circa 1964

Official Dutch Beatles' cotton dress in mustard with polka dots. With the makers' card tag.
- £395
- More Than Music

Heavy Metal
- circa 1977

Issue no. 1 of *Heavy Metal* magazine, pursuivant on the cult film of the same name.
- £20
- Book & Comic Exchange

Beatles Talc Powder
- 1964

Talcum powder tin with different studies of the loveable mop-tops on either side. By Margo of Mayfair.
- height 18cm
- £450
- More Than Music

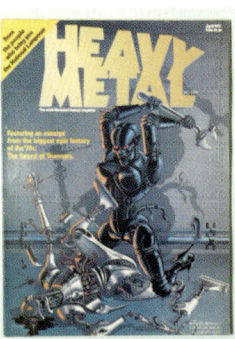

Portrait by Joe Meek
- circa 1966

"Pat as I see Him" – pen and ink on envelope by producer Joe Meek of his boyfriend.
- £5,950
- Music & Video

Expert Tips

The more recent the star, the more memorabilia will have been made to support them. There is very little Buddy Holly ephemera about, but a great deal on the Spice Girls.

Harrison Autobiography
- 1980

Rare, unsigned hardback copy of first edition of Beatle George Harrison's autobiography *I Me Mine*, with dust cover. Published by Simon Schuster.
- £75
- More Than Music

Rock & Pop

Official Carded Beatles Accessories
- *1964*
Sales cards containing Beatles cufflinks and tie-pin, with the group's heads cast in brass.
- £245 (left), £175 (right)
- More Than Music

Official Carded Jewellery Box
- *1964*
Oval leather and brass accessories, with The Beatles' faces featured on the lid of the box.
- £225   • More Than Music

The Who Album
- *1965*
The Who's *My Generation* album, by Brunswick, with original band line-up on cover. Poor condition.
- £40   • Music & Video

Official Corgi Toy
- *1968*
Die-cast metal yellow submarine with revolving periscope and one yellow and one white hatch. From the movie.
- £375   • More Than Music

Official Brooch
- *1964*
Official Nicki Byrne-designed Beatles brooch, with guitar and drum interwoven with the group's name and ceramic plaque showing their image, all on the original sales card.
- £250   • More Than Music

Expert Tips

There was much more scope for worthwhile artwork on the vinyl album covers of the 60s and 70s than on the subsequent cassette and compact disk covers. This is reflected in the prices of original artwork of the period.

Beatles Sneakers
- *circa 1964*
Official "Wing Dings" Beatles sneakers, with images and signatures of the group on the shoes and the original box. In excellent condition.
- £795   • More Than Music

93

Rock & Pop

Siouxsie and The Banshees Memorabilia ➤
- 1981
Half-page artwork for promotion of the *Arabian Knights* tour by Siouxsie and the Banshees.
- 40cm x 35cm
- £175 • Music & Video

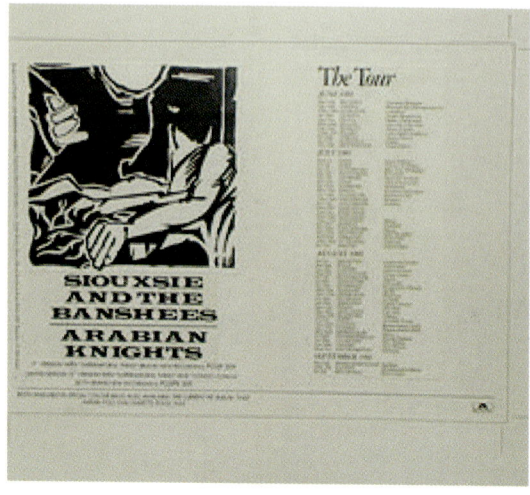

Bruce Springsteen Single ▲
- 1981
"Cadillac Ranch" single by Bruce Springsteen.
- 18cm x 18cm
- £25 • Music & Video

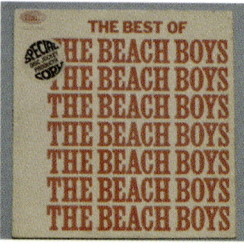

Beach Boys Album ▲
- circa 1966
Special disc jockey/producer copy of *The Best of the Beach Boys* album, released by EMI Records, London.
- £184 • Music & Video

The Police Singles Box ▲
- 1990
Embossed wooden box containing 10 gold vinyl singles together with a picture disc by The Police.
- 18cm x 18cm
- £195 • Music & Video

Manic Street Preachers Single ◄
- 1988
Double A-side single "Suicide Alley Tennessee" containing a letter from the band.
- 18cm x 18cm
- £995 • Music & Video

Rock & Pop

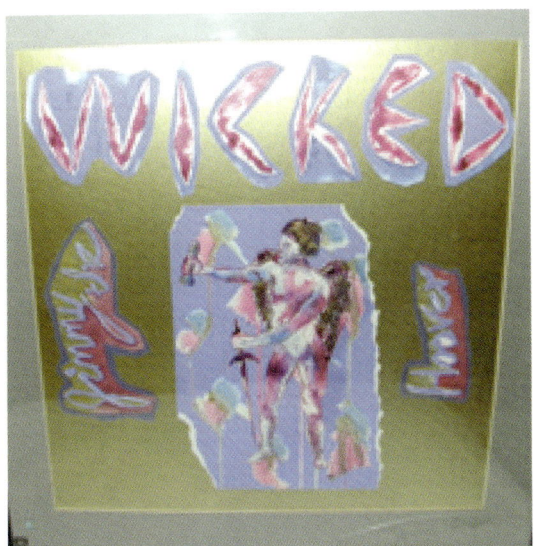

Album Artwork
- 1984

Unused album artwork for Jimmy the Hoover by Jamie Reid, with glass broken and damaged intentionally for the "Leaving the 21st Century" series held at the Mayfair gallery.
- 50cm x 50cm
- £200   • Music & Video

4AD Calendar
- 1993

Collector's item calendar issued by record company, 4AD, and designed by 23 Envelope.
- 35cm x 55cm
- £25   • Music & Video

Brute Force Album featuring John Lennon
- 1970

Extemporaneous album by Brute Force featuring John Lennon.
- £395   • Music & Video

Withdrawn Single
- 1981

"Ha ha I'm drowning" single by The Teardrop Explodes. Withdrawn issue.
- 18cm x 18cm
- £60   • Music & Video

Wing's Record Sleeve
- 1975

Record sleeve for Wing's "Listen to what the man said" and "King Alfred's Rubbish", autographed by Paul and Linda McCartney.
- £675   • More Than Music

Rolling Stones Album
- 1971

Copy of the Rolling Stones album *Sticky Fingers*.
- 30cm x 30cm
- £240   • Music & Video

Scripophilly & Paper Money

> ### Expert Tips
> *Printing errors, rarity of production and condition are all important when buying paper money but watch out for those forgeries as they can end up costing you money!*

New Orleans Note
- *circa 1860*
New Orleans $20 note issued by Canal Bank.
- £12.50
- C. Narbeth

Confederate States Note
- *1864*
Confederate States $10 note issued in the US Civil War.
- £28
- C. Narbeth

National Currency 20 Dollar Note
- *1900*
$20 note issued by the Citizen's Bank of Eureka, Kansas, during the Battle of Lexington.
- £595
- C. Narbeth

Military Payment Note
- *1970*
Military payment certificate to the value of 10 cents.
- £6
- C. Narbeth

Colonial Note
- *1773*
Colonial 15 shillings note issued in Pennsylvania. Numbered and signed by hand.
- £48
- C. Narbeth

American Note
- *1995*
American note to the amount of $2.
- £3
- C. Narbeth

Scripophilly & Paper Money

500 Rouble Note
- *1912*

A large Russian 500 rouble note, showing a portrait of Peter the Great. In extremely fine condition.
- £5
- C. Narbeth

Hungarian Pengo Note
- *1946*

100,000 billion pengo note – reflecting the world's highest ever inflation in post-war Hungary. In extremely fine condition.
- £3.50
- C. Narbeth

Boer War Note
- *1900*

A South African Boer War note of five pounds, issued from Pretoria, the Boer capital. In very fine condition.
- £28
- C. Narbeth

Three Pence Note
- *circa 1960*

A British Armed Forces three pence note, mainly for use by the British Army of the Rhine in Germany.
- £12.50
- C. Narbeth

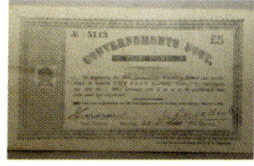

Letter from Edward VII
- *18th January 1910*

A crested letter and photo regarding his private affairs. Addressed to his sister-in-law, the Duchess of Connaught, and sent from Sandringham.
- £650
- Jim Hanson

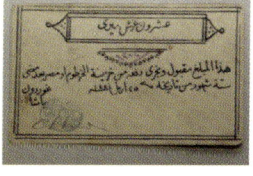

Siege of Khartoum Note
- *circa 1884*

A 20 piastre note from the siege of Khartoum, Sudan. Hand-signed by General Gordon and in very fine condition.
- £275
- C. Narbeth

Squad Photograph
- *1966*

Signed, commemorative photograph of the England 1966 World Cup winning team, featuring Alf Ramsey, the team manager, Bobby Moore, the captain and players Nobby Stiles and Martin Peters, with signatures of the entire winning team. A full squad photograph is also included.
- £2,500
- Star Signings

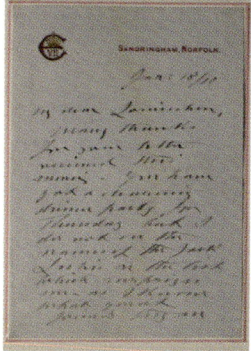

Chinese Cash Note
- *circa 1858*

A Chinese 2,000 cash note issued during the Taiping Rebellion. In very fine condition.
- £65
- C. Narbeth

Tibetan Note
- circa 1950

A 100 strang denomination note from Tibet, serial numbers applied by hand by Buddhist monks. One seal represents the monetary authority and the other that of the Dalai Lama. Uncirculated.
- £22
- C. Narbeth

Letter from George V
- 19th October 1873

Written by the future king, then aged eight, from Marlborough House, to Lady Julia Lockwood.
- £650
- Jim Hanson

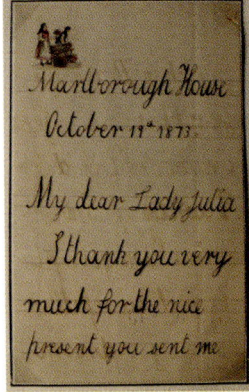

Swedish Kronor
- 1940

A Swedish five kronor note. Extremely fine.
- £9.50
- C. Narbeth

Austrian 1,000 Kronen
- 1919

An Austrian tausend Kronen note in mint condition.
- £3.50
- C. Narbeth

African Republic Note
- circa 1974

A 500 franc note from the Central African Republic, showing President Bokassa in a military pose. In mint condition.
- £70
- C. Narbeth

Five Reichsmark Note
- circa 1942

Dated from the Second World War and showing a Hitler Youth in the Horst Wessel mould.
- £10
- C. Narbeth

Fifty Mark Note
- circa 1933

A German 50 mark note. Extremely fine condition.
- £3.50
- C. Narbeth

Expert Tips

Check that the four corners of a note are sharp; hold it up to the light to check for creases; if it curls in the palm of the hand, it has been ironed.

Ugandan Bank Note
- circa 1973

An Idi Amin Ugandan bank note of five shillings' value. Extremely fine note.
- £4.50
- C. Narbeth

Scripophilly & Paper Money

Bank of England Note
- 1972
£20 note bearing a portrait of Queen Elizabeth II.
- £1972
- C. Narbeth

Fijiian Treasury Note
- 12th July 1873
Treasury note in the amount of £50, issued in Fiji.
- £495
- C. Narbeth

US Railway Bond
- 1881
$500 dollar bond issued by the Indiana Coal and Railway Co.
- £35
- C. Narbeth

Railway Bond
- 1911
Bond issued by the Brazil Railway Company.
- £18
- C. Narbeth

English Note
- 1950
White £5 note issued by the Bank of England.
- £89.50
- C. Narbeth

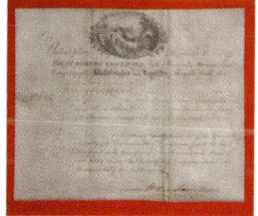

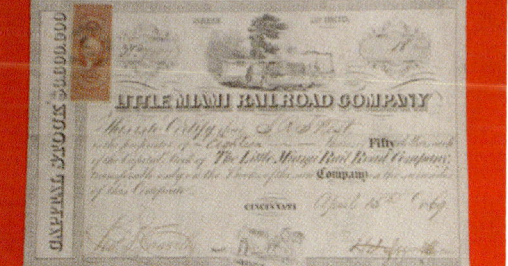

Signed US Share
- 1895
Philadelphia and Lancaster share signed "Bingham". Early US share with a vignette.
- £795
- C. Narbeth

Railroad Shares
- 1864
Share issued by the Little Miami Railroad Company.
- £10
- C. Narbeth

English Banknote
- 1987
English £50 note signed by David Somerset.
- £95
- C. Narbeth

Russian Note
- 1884
Russian 10 rouble note issued in the reign of Czar Alexander III.
- £850
- C. Narbeth

Chinese Bond
- *1911*
£20 bond issued by the Imperial Chinese Government.
- £65
- C. Narbeth

Portuguese Bond
- *1922*
Bond issued by the Companhia Colonial Navegaedo.
- £7
- C. Narbeth

Iraqi Note
- *1931*
ID 1 banknote, numbered A 157545, from Iraq.
- £450
- C. Narbeth

Swiss Note
- *1952*
SFr 5 note issued by the national bank of Switzerland.
- £38
- C. Narbeth

British Linen Co. Note
- *18th January 1896*
£5 note issued by the British Linen Company.
- £325
- C. Narbeth

Expert Tips

The first European banknote was printed in Scandinavia in 1661. Since then a wealth of paper money has been issued. Keep your eyes on bank notes as they are likely to become a worthwhile investment.

Irish Banknote
- *1977*
£50 note issued by The Central Bank of Ireland.
- £175
- C. Narbeth

Bolivian Note
- *1928*
$b1 note issued by the Central Bank of Bolivia.
- £4
- C. Narbeth

Scottish Pound Note
- *1969*
£1 note issued by the Bank of Scotland.
- £25
- C. Narbeth

Sewing Items

Sewing Table
- *circa 1840*
A lyre-ended chinoiserie sewing table of the 19th-century.
- *height 65cm*
- £750   • North West 8

Needle Case
- *circa 1890*
Ivory and mother-of-pearl needle case with hinged lid and silver cornucopia.
- *length 7.5cm*
- £149   • Fulham

Regency Table Cabinet
- *circa 1815*
Shaped late-Regency table cabinet in rosewood, with mother-of-pearl inlay and fitted sewing tray.
- *width 32.5cm*
- £1,800   • Hygra

Tunbridge Ware
- *circa 1800*
A turned and painted early Tunbridge-ware sewing companion.
- *height 6cm*
- £450   • Hygra

Small Sewing Machine
- *circa 1900*
An American "Little Comfort", handle-driven sewing machine.
- *height 17.5cm*
- £350   • TalkMach

Work Table
- *circa 1850*
Scandinavian birchwood work table. With turned, adjustable central column.
- *height 1.1m*
- £995   • Old Cinema

Compartmentalised Thread Box
- *circa 1810*
A straw-work thread box.
- *width 44cm*
- £180   • Hygra

Sewing Items

Carpet Sticher
- *19th century*
An American hand-powered carpet stitcher made by the Singer factory.
- *length 59cm*
- £285 • Mathews

Sewing Box ▼
- *circa 1800*
Early 19th-century sewing box in pollarded oak and rosewood inlay. Retaining its original lift-out tray.
- *width 28cm*
- £480 • Hygra

Bobbins ▲
- *circa 1930*
Selection of three fruitwood bobbins with beaded decoration and carved stems.
- *length 19cm*
- £4 each • Mathews

Chinese Sewing Box ▼
- *circa 1820*
Sewing box in Chinese lacquer. The box stands on four carved wooden feet. Chinese-made for export to England.
- *width 42.5cm*
- £1,200 • Hygra

Necessaire ▲
- *circa 1780*
An 18th-century tortoiseshell and silver necessaire.
- *height 7.5cm*
- £1,200 • Hygra

Sewing Basket ▲
- *early 19th century*
A fine and delicate Anglo-Indian sewing basket, with fretted ivory panels framed with Sadeli mosaic.
- *width 20cm*
- £1,200 • Hygra

> ## Expert Tips
>
> *Thomas Saint patented the world's first sewing machine in 1790, in England.*

Miniature Singer ▶
- *circa 1935*
A cast-iron Singer sewing machine of the Art Deco period, hand-driven and with a raised action and bobbin board.
- *height 13cm*
- £400 • TalkMach

Sewing Items

Hardwood Sewing Box
- circa 1775
An eighteenth-century sewing box with native and imported hardwoods juxtaposed and a neo-classical central motif.
- width 29cm
- £720 • Hygra

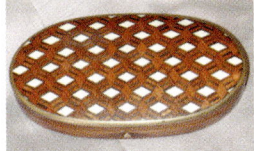

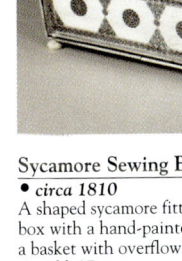

Kingwood Sewing Box ▲
- 1830
Kingwood sewing box inlaid with ivory in a diamond pattern, enclosing silver gilt needlework tools.
- length 10cm
- £490 • Thimble Society

Rosewood Sewing Box ▲
- circa 1835
Fully fitted rosewood and mother-of-pearl sewing box labelled "George Johnston Glasgow".
- width 31cm
- £1,800 • Hygra

Inlaid Sewing Box ▼
- 1820
Very fine early nineteenth century Anglo-Indian ivory and sadeli mosaic fitted sewing box.
- width 32cm
- £950 • Hygra

Expert Tips

When buying sewing machines try to look out for the smaller versions, for example a miniature Singer or the "Little Comfort", an American-made sewing machine, as these tend to be more expensive than their larger counterparts. For those who would like to collect smaller items the necessaires and thimbles, especially from the Elizabethan period are very expensive, although anything pre-eighteenth century will still command a good price.

Silver Thimbles ▲
- mid-19th century
A selection of three silver thimbles with intricate silver skirts set with coloured stones.
- height 2.6cm
- £90 each • Thimble Society

Sycamore Sewing Box ▼
- circa 1810
A shaped sycamore fitted sewing box with a hand-painted design of a basket with overflowing flowers.
- width 27cm
- £1,800 • Hygra

Regency Sewing Box ▼
- 1835
Regency rosewood sewing box of sarcophagus form with pewter stringing, gadroon bordering, and lozenge feet. The interior with original red velvet and silk lining. The box contains a letter dated 1843, probably from the original owner.
- 16cm x 33cm x 26cm
- £995 • J. & T. Stone

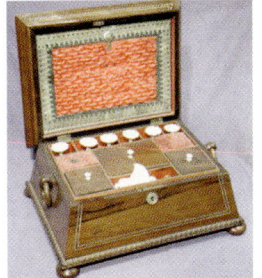

Snuff Boxes & Smoking Equipment

Monkey Snuff Box
- *circa 1800*
Finely carved snuffbox in the shape of a monkey.
- *height 7cm*
- £950 • A. & E. Foster

Horn Snuff Mull
- *circa 1810*
Extremely rare silver-mounted horn snuff mull. Made by Robert Kaye of Perth, Scotland.
- *length 15cm*
- £1,750 • Nicholas Shaw

Expert Tips

If a snuff box or similar item is to be engraved, then it is best if it is engraved in favour of a famous person or event. Items with re-engraving or erasing are considered damaged.

Spitfire Ashtray
- *circa 1950*
Spitfire brass trophy ashtray. On marble base. Spitfire with pivot support.
- *height 15cm*
- £90 • Henry Gregory

Match Strike
- *circa 1900*
Glass circular match strike with incised banding around outer edge for striking.
- *height 12cm*
- £98 • Magpies

Wooden Snuffbox
- *circa 1860*
Handcarved Scottish snuffbox.
- *length 6cm*
- *height 6cm*
- £1,250 • The Lacquer Chest

Cigar Cutter
- *circa 1880*
Ivory and silver cigar cutter. Monogrammed. No marks.
- *length 15cm*
- £420 • S. & A. Thompson

Cigarette Box
- *circa 1940*
Silver cigarette box with 18ct gold sides. Smooth with a small lip. By Boucheron, Paris.
- £2,000 • Henry Gregory

Goat Head Snuff Box
- *late 19th century*
Snuff box in the shape of a goat's head. Pewter fittings. Brown and blue glaze with grey horns.
- *height 13cm*
- £1,100 • Elizabeth Bradwin

Snuff Boxes & Smoking Equipment

Gold and Tortoiseshell Snuff Box
- *1702*

Queen Anne gold and tortoiseshell snuff box made in London. The lid inset with a gold coin commemorating Queen Anne's coronation. One of 750 that were issued at the time.
- *length 8cm*
- £4,250   • N. Shaw

Silver Vesta Case
- *1926*

A silver George V vesta case made in London by The Goldsmith and Silversmith Company Ltd.
- *length 3cm*
- £675   • N. Shaw

Novelty Vesta Case
- *1888*

A silver Victorian novelty vesta case.
- *length 6cm*
- £575   • N. Shaw

Austrian Snuff Box
- *1924*

An Austrian snuff box with indigo enamel on a tooled silver base, with pierced floral cartouches in a neo-classical style.
- *length 8cm*
- £480   • Thimble Society

Silver Gilt Snuff Box
- *1855*

A Victorian silver gilt snuff box presented to Captain H. G. Kennedy of the ship *Parker*. Made by Edward Smith in Birmingham
- *length 11cm*
- £2,250   • N. Shaw

Mahogany Snuff Box
- *1860*

Mahogany shoe inlaid with brass design and mother of pearl.
- *6cm x 9cm*
- £525   • Bill Chapman

Snuff Boxes & Smoking Equipment

Cigar Box
- 1920

Unusual burr walnut cigar and cigarette box with gilded handle and decoration. Two lighter drawers with match strikers.
- width 24cm
- £495   • J. & T. Stone

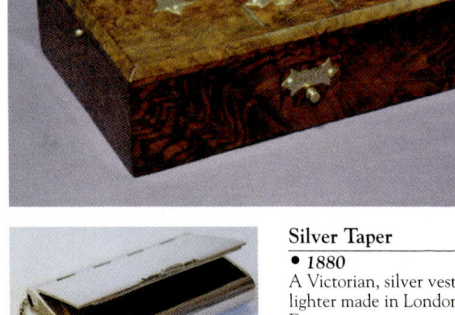

Silver Taper
- 1880

A Victorian, silver vesta/ taper lighter made in London by Louis Dee.
- length 11cm
- £650   • N. Shaw

Continental Vesta Case
- circa 1900

A continental vesta case decorated with an enamel chestnut horse's head.
- 3cm
- £450   • N. Shaw

George IV Snuff Box
- 1822–23

A George IV snuff box made in Birmingham by Joseph Willmore.
- length 4cm
- £450   • N. Shaw

Victorian Snuff Box
- 1840

A silver Victorian snuff box with an oak leaf pattern, presented to Mr William McKelvic of Redruth.
- length 3.5cm
- £2,750   • N. Shaw

Expert Tips

Cigarette boxes are extremely collectable, especially the examples from the Art Deco period. Their value also increases if they are made from gold or silver and carry a hallmark. When purchasing these items it is important that one bears in mind the craftsmanship and style of the piece. Early cigar cutters will always command a high price, and any snuff box with a zoographical theme is always worth buying.

Double Snuff Box
- 1858

A George IV double Regi Mari snuff box inscribed, "London 1827, Tria Juncta In Uno. Presented by Lieut Col Caulfield and the Married Officers of the mess of the 33rd Roscommon Regiment, 17 March 1858". Engraved with a four-leaf clover.
- length 6cm
- £3,950   • N. Shaw

Telephones

Series 700 Telephone ▲
- *circa 1967*
British Telecom, acrylic with rotary dial, flexicord and handset extension. Resprayed in silver.
- £85 • After Noah

Viscount Telephone ▼
- *circa 1986*
A British Telecom-supplied telephone in burnt orange with cream flexcord extension.
- £20 • Retro

Swiss Telephone ▲
- *circa 1950*
A Swiss wall-mounted telephone with bell-ring displayed to top and hook connection.
- £100 • Decodence

Bakelite Telephone ▼
- *circa 1950*
A GPO model telephone cast in bakelite with rotary dial.
- £125 • H. Hay

Elvis Presley Telephone ▲
- *circa 1980*
"Jailhouse Rock" shown with guitar and period clothes. Touch tone handset.
- £99 • Telephone Lines

Danish Telephone ▲
- *circa 1935*
A Danish magneto telephone based on an L.M. Ericsson design. Can't be used on today's system.
- £270 • Old Telephone Co

Expert Tips

Collectors should be careful to keep old bakelite telephones out of direct sunlight, the greatest enemy of antiques. It fades them irreversibly.

Upright Dial Telephone ▶
- *circa 1908*
Made from 1908 by Telefon Fabrik Automatic of Copenhagen.
- £510 • Old Telephone Co

Telephones

Betacom "Golphone"
- *mid-1980*

Model GFI. Made in Hong Kong with golf-bag handset and push buttons, mute tone and redial.
- £18   • Retro

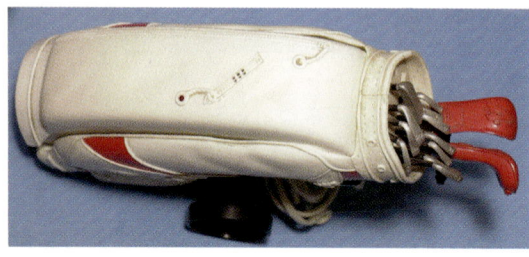

> **Expert Tips**
>
> The best polish for use on telephones is hard beeswax. The advantage that this has over silicone polishes is that the latter tend to make phones slippery and easy to drop.

Danish Telephone
- *circa 1930*

Telephone with dial and hand-raised cradle, made in Denmark for the Danish telephone authority.
- £350   • Old Telephone Co

Belgian Wall Phone
- *circa 1960*

A Belgian wall phone repainted in red. Made in Antwerp by Bell Telephones, a subsidiary of the American Bell Telephones.
- £180   • Old Telephone Co

500 Series Telephone
- *circa 1978*

Made by Northern Telecom, Stromberg-Carlson. Originally supplied for an American airforce base but resold in 1994. Unused and in original sealed box.
- £95   • Old Telephone Co

300 Series Telephone
- *circa 1955*

A 300 series black bakelite office telephone with original handset, cord and draw.
- £230   • Old Telephone Co

Audioline 310 Telephone
- *circa 1980*

Red Audioline 310, with oversized keypad with numbers also in red, push-button controls and black flexicord extension.
- £30   • Retro

R2D2 Telephone
- *circa 1980*

A telephone in the form of the character R2D2, from the *Star Wars* films. His head moves and lifts up when the phone rings.
- £99   • Telephone Lines

Telephones

Ivory Telephone ▶
- *circa 1930*
A GPO telephone in ivory, rare for the period. Shows all-metal rotary dial with original central label and number/letter display.
- £395   • H. Hay

Danish Telephone ▲
- *circa 1935*
A variation on the D30, with two exchange lines coming in. Supplied with a separate bell set.
- £420   • Old Telephone Co

Desk Telephone ▲
- *circa 1960*
A Belgian desk telephone in black plastic, with black rotary dial and white base on rubber feet.
- £150   • Old Telephone Co

Magneto Telephone ▼
- *circa 1925*
A classic design by L. M. Ericsson, Stockholm, made from around 1896. Also known as Eiffel Tower.
- £850   • Old Telephone Co

300 Series Telephone ▲
- *circa 1954*
By Siemens Brothers, Woolwich. Rarest colour in this series. Used for shared or party lines.
- £600   • Old Telephone Co

Darth Vader Telephone ◀
- *circa 1980*
Telephone in the form of Darth Vader, from *Star Wars*, with moving head.
- £99   • Telephone Lines

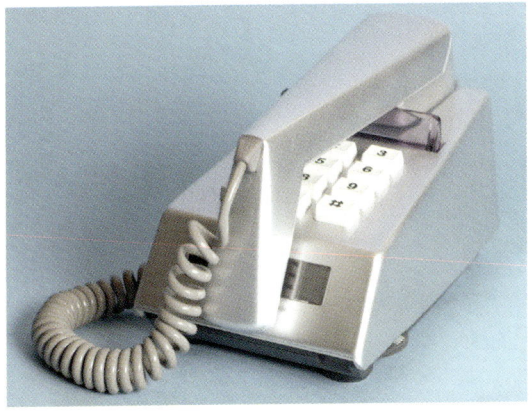

Expert Tips

Ascertain from the dealer, when effecting your purchase, whether the telephone you are buying can be used on a modern system and, if so, what conversion equipment is necessary.

Trimphone ◀
- *circa 1970*
Silver-painted British "Trimphone" made for the GPO, with push-button dialling. With distinctive ringing tone.
- £85   • After Noah

Queen's Silver Jubilee
- *circa 1977*

Very rare and limited edition, unused with type 64d bell set. Introduced to commemorate the 25th year of Elizabeth II's reign.
- £150
- Old Telephone Co

Ericofon Telephone
- *circa 1955*

Designed in 1953 by Ralph Lysell and Hugo Blomberg. In white and red with dial underneath.
- £70
- Telephone Lines Ltd

Bakelite Pyramid Phone
- *circa 1930*

Series 200 with chrome rotary dial, cloth flex and address drawer.
- £295
- After Noah

Model 1000
- *circa 1962*

Made by GEC of Coventry and was intended as a replacement for the 300 series but not adopted.
- £160
- Old Telephone Co

300 Series Telephone
- *circa 1957*

A rare 328 telephone made by Plessey, Ilford, Essex. With bell-on and bell-off push buttons.
- £650
- Old Telephone Co

Candlestick Telephone
- *circa 1927*

Type 150, in bakelite, featuring a replacement microphone. Made by Ibex Telephones.
- £460
- Old Telephone Co

Expert Tips

Telephones do not have to work in order to be collectable. Very early ones are intrinsically valuable as are some of the antiques of the future – early mobiles and car-phones.

Genie Telephone
- *circa 1978*

BT special range, a much sought-after designer telephone in white with metal dial.
- £39
- Telephone Lines Ltd

Telephones

Black Plastic Telephone
- *1960*
Black plastic telephone with white letters and numbers, and black flex.
- *13cm x 13cm x 21cm*
- £55 • Radio Days

Ericsson Telephone
- *circa 1905*
A Swedish-made, Ericsson, wooden wall-mounted phone with bell-ring display to top.
- *69cm x 26cm*
- £495 • Telephone Lines

Series 300 Telephone
- *1940s–1950s*
An English acrylic golden yellow telephone with drawer for addresses and integral bell.
- *19cm x 18cm*
- £300 • Decodence

Candlestick Telephone
- *1916*
French candlestick telephone with metal and chrome handset and wooden candlestick base by Grammont.
- *height 34cm*
- £615 • Telephone Lines

Desk Telephone
- *1895*
A Dutch wooden desk phone with rotary dial.
- *height 15cm*
- £295 • Telephone Lines

Expert Tips

Even if a phone is termed a novelty phone this does not imply that it is of low worth. Bear in mind that these will be the collectables of the future and will increase in value as the years go by, just remember to keep the original box!

Walking Sticks

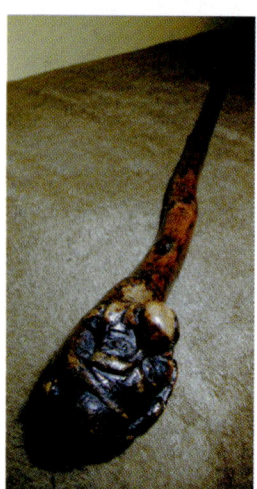

Wooden Cane
- circa 1890
Gargoyle head on a gnarled wooden cane.
- 92cm x 6cm x 3cm
- £240 • Henry Gregory

Whalebone Cane
- circa 1840
A fine whalebone cane with full barley twist shaft. The whale handle loop carved with a serpent's head.
- length 70cm
- £1,600 • Michael German

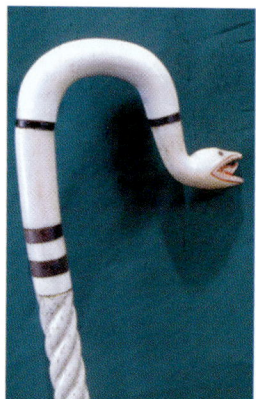

City Walking Cane
- circa 1900
Ebonised cane with gioche enamel ball, gold band and Austrian mark.
- length 55cm
- £750 • Michael German

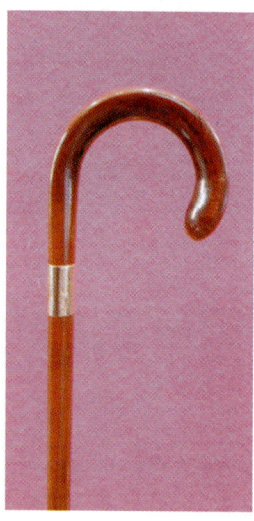

Snakewood Walking Cane
- circa 1900
An elegant, rare snakewood cane with gold collar and looped handle.
- length 89cm
- £550 • Michael German

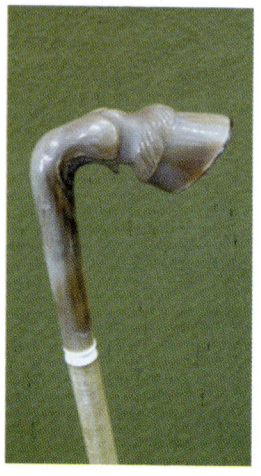

Hoof Walking Stick
- circa 1880
Carved horn hoof handle mounted on unusual segmented shaft formed from paper washers.
- length 100cm/handle
- £650 • Michael German

Japanese Walking Cane
- circa 1900
Japanese bamboo cane inset with ivory face and silver collar.
- length 20cm
- £680 • Michael German

Walking Sticks

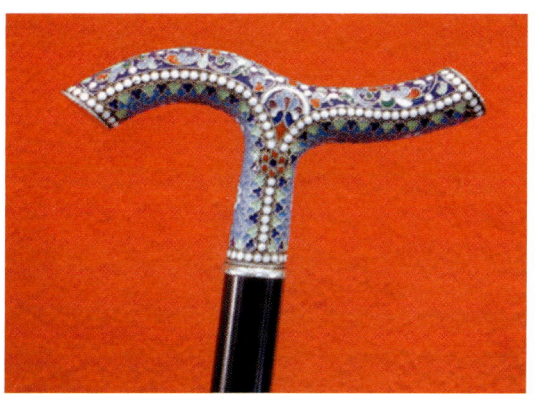

Carved Walking Stick
- circa 1860
Folk art cane with deeply carved animals, trees and fruit, silver collar and rounded top.
- length 92cm
- £925   • Michael German

Russian Walking Cane
- circa 1890
Russian ebonised cane with an elaborately decorated silver handle with overlaid enamel Tau and Russian marks
- length 90cm
- £1,400   • Michael German

Cricket Ball Walking Stick
- circa 1870
Unusual folk art cane with hand holding cricket ball, carved shaft.
- length 100cm
- £480   • Michael German

Expert Tips

Items related to personalities plus the Royal connection are especially popular. Walking sticks were a playground for the craftsman. Some were hollowed out and fitted with stem like decanters, others with swords, horse measuring sticks or even to conceal a gun. Perhaps those most sought after are those with beautifully carved ivory grips, or those with a zoographical theme.

Elephant Walking Cane
- circa 1890
Ebonised cane with an ivory baby elephant with glass eyes, in a seated position.
- length 78cm
- £1,200   • Michael German

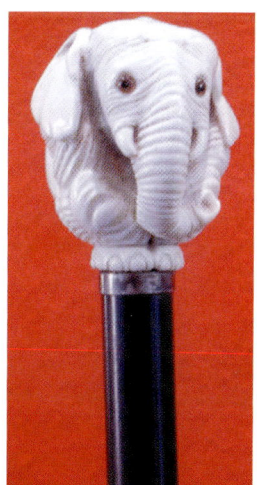

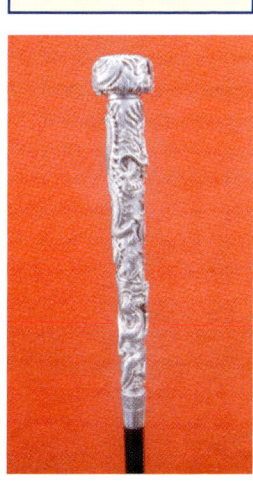

Chinese Walking Cane
- circa 1880–90
An ornate silver cane from China with a long silver handle chased with a dragon design.
- length 100cm
- £680   • Michael German

Directory of Dealers

There follows a list of antique dealers, many of whom have provided items in the main body of the book and all of whom will be happy to assist within their areas of expertise.

Abacus Antiques
(ref: Abacus)
Grays Antiques Market,
58 Davies Street, London W1Y 2LP
Tel: 020 7629 9681

Antiques.

After Noah
121 Upper Street,
London N1 8ED
Tel: 020 7359 4281
Fax: 020 7359 4281
www.afternoah.com

Antique furniture, linen and postcards.

After Noah (Kings Road)
(ref: After Noah (KR))
261 Kings Road,
London SW3 5EL
Tel: 020 7351 2610
Fax: 020 7351 2610
www.afternoah.com

Antique furniture, linen and postcards.

Albany Antiques
(ref: Albany)
8–10 London Road, Hindhead,
Surrey GU26 6AF
Tel: 01428 605 528
Fax: 01428 605 528

Georgian furniture, eighteenth-century brass, Victorian antiques, porcelain and statuary.

Armoury of St James, The
(ref: The Armoury)
17 Piccadilly Arcade,
London SW1Y 6NH
Tel: 020 7493 5083
Fax: 020 7499 4422
www.armoury.co.uk/home

Royal memorabilia and model soldiers.

Victor Arwas Gallery
(ref: Arwas)
3 Clifford Street,
London W1X 1RA
Tel: 020 7734 3944
Fax: 020 7437 1859
www.victorarwas.com

Art Nouveau and Art Deco, glass, ceramics, bronzes, sculpture, furniture, jewellery, silver, pewter, books and posters, from 1880–1940. Paintings, watercolours and drawings, 1880 to date. Original graphics, lithographs, etchings and woodcuts from 1890 to date.

Linda Bee
Grays in the Mews Antiques Market,
1–7 Davies Mews,
London W1Y 1AR
Tel: 020 7629 5921
Fax: 020 7629 5921

Vintage costume jewellery and fashion accessories.

Beverley
30 Church Street,
Marylebone,
London NW8 8EP
Tel: 020 7262 1576
Fax: 020 7262 1576

English ceramics, glass, metal, wood, pottery, collectables and decorative items from 1850–1950.

Book and Comic Exchange
(ref: Book & Comic)
14 Pembridge Road,
London W11 3HL
Tel: 020 7229 8420
www.buy-sell-trade.co.uk

Modern first editions, cult books and comics.

Malcolm Bord Gold Coin Exchange
(ref: Malcolm Bord)
16 Charing Cross Road,
London WC2 0HR
Tel: 020 7836 0631/020 7240 0479/
020 7240 1920

Dealing in all types of coin, medal and bank note.

Directory of Dealers

Elizabeth Bradwin
75 Portobello Road,
London W11 2QB
Tel: 020 7221 1121
Fax: 020 8947 2629
www.elizabethbradwin.com

Animal subjects.

Bridge Bikes
137 Putney Bridge,
London SW15 2PA
Tel: 020 8870 3934

Bikes.

Jasmin Cameron
Antiquarias Antiques Market,
135 Kings Road,
London SW3 4PW
Tel: 020 7351 4154
Fax: 020 7351 4154

Drinking glasses and decanters 1750–1910, vintage fountain pens and writing materials. **C. A. R. S. of Brighton**

(ref: C. A. R. S.)
4–4a Chapel Terrace Mews,
Kemp Town, Brighton BN2 1HU
Tel: 01273 622 722
Fax: 01273 601 960
www.carsofbrighton.co.uk

Classic automobilia and regalia specialists, and children's pedal cars.

Cartoon Gallery, The
(ref: Cartoon Gallery)
39 Great Russell Street,
London WC1 3PH
Tel: 020 7636 1011
Fax: 020 7436 5053

Comics.

Mia Cartwright Antiques
(ref: Mia Cartwright)
20th C. Theatre Arcade,
291 Westbourne Grove (Sats),
London W11
Tel: 01273 579100

Bill Chapman
Shop No. 11, Bourbon/
Hanby Antique Centre,
151 Sydney Street,
London SW3 6NT
Tel: 020 7351 5387

Collectables.

Chelsea Military Antiques
(ref: Chelsea (OMRS))
Stands N13–14, Antiquarius,
131–141 Kings Road,
London SW3 4PW
Tel: 020 7352 0308
Fax: 020 7352 0308
www.chelseamilitaria.co.uk

Pre-1945 militaria, edge weapons, medals including British and foreign campaign/gallantry medals.

John Clay Antiques
(ref: John Clay)
263 New Kings Road,
London SW6 4RB
Tel: 020 7731 5677

Furniture, objets d'art, silver and clocks from the eighteenth and nineteenth century.

Cobwebs
73 Avery Hill Road, New Eltham,
London SE9 2BJ
Tel: 020 8850 5611

Furniture, general antiques and collectables.

Garrick D. Coleman
(ref: G. D. Coleman)
75 Portobello Road,
London W11 2QB
Tel: 020 7937 5524
Fax: 020 7937 5530
www.antiquechess.co.uk

Antiques, fine chess sets and glass paperweights.

Rosemary Conquest
(ref: R. Conquest)
4 Charlton Place,
London N1 8AJ
Tel: 020 7359 0616

Continental and Dutch lighting, copper, brass and decorative items.

Curios Gardens & Interiors
(ref: Curios)
130c Junction Road,
Tufnell Park,
London N19 5LB
Tel: 020 7272 5603
Fax: 020 7272 5603

Garden furniture, statuary, reclaimed pine furniture and antique furniture.

Directory of Dealers

Decodence
21 The Mall,
359 Upper Street,
London N1 0PD
Tel: 020 7354 4473
Fax: 020 7689 0680

Classic plastics such as bakelite, celluloid and catalin; vintage radios, lighting, telephones and toys.

Dodo
Stand Fo73, Alfie's Antiques Market,
13–25 Church Street,
London NW8 8DT
Tel: 020 7706 1545
Fax: 020 7724 0999

Posters, tins and advertising signs, 1890–1940.

Drummonds Architectural Antiques Ltd
(ref: Drummonds)
The Kirkpatrick Buildings,
25 London Road, Hindhead,
Surrey GU26 6AB
Tel: 01428 609444
Fax: 01428 609445
www.drummonds-arch.co.uk

Restored original and new bathrooms, reclaimed wood and stone flooring, fireplaces, statues, garden features, lighting, gates and railings, doors and door furniture, radiators, antique furniture, windows and large architectural features.

A. & E. Foster
Little Heysham, Forge Road, Naphill,
Buckinghamshire HP14 4SU
Tel: 01494 562024
Fax: 01494 562024

Antique treen works of art and early treen.

Fulham Antiques
(ref: Fulham)
320 Munster Road,
London SW6 6BH
Tel: 020 7610 3644
Fax: 020 7610 3644

Antique and decorative furniture, lighting and mirrors.

G Whizz
17 Jerdan Place,
London SW6 1BE
Tel: 020 7386 5020
Fax: 020 8741 0062
www.metrocycle.co.uk

Bikes.

Michael German Antiques
(ref: Michael German)
38b Kensington Church Street,
London W8 4BX
Tel: 020 7937 2771
Fax: 020 7937 8566
www.antiquecanes.com
www.antiqueweapons.com

Antique walking canes, antique arms and armour.

Gabrielle de Giles
The Barn at Bilsington,
Swanton Lane, Bilsington,
Ashford, Kent TN25 7JR
Tel: 01233 720917
Fax: 01233 720156

Antique and country furniture, home interiors, designer for curtains and screens.

Gosh
39 Great Russell Street,
London WC1B 3PH
Tel: 020 7436 5053
Fax: 020 7436 5053

Henry Gregory
82 Portobello Road,
London W11 2QD
Tel: 020 7792 9221
Fax: 020 7792 9221

Silver-plate, silver, sporting goods and decorative antiques.

Jim Hanson & Argyll Etkin Ltd
18 Claremont Field,
Ottery St Mary,
Devon EX11 1NP
Tel: 01404 815010
Fax: 01404 815224

Philatelist and postal historian.

Keith Harding's World of Mechanical Music
(ref: Keith Harding)
The Oak House,
High Street, Northleach,
Gloucestershire GL54 3ET
Tel: 01451 860181
Fax: 01451 861133
www.mechanicalmusic.co.uk

Gerard Hawthorn Ltd
(ref: Gerard Hawthorn)
104 Mount Street,
London W1Y 5HE
Tel: 020 7409 2888
Fax: 020 7409 2777

Chinese, Japanese and Korean ceramics and works of art.

Directory of Dealers

Henry Hay
Unit 5054, 2nd floor,
Alfie's Market, 13–25 Church Street,
London NW8
Tel: 020 7723 2548

Art Deco and twentieth-century chrome and brass lamps and bakelite telephones.

Holland & Holland
31–33 Bruton Street,
London W1X 8JS
Tel: 020 7499 4411
Fax: 020 7409 3283

Guns.

Hope & Glory
131a Kensington Church Street
(entrance in Peel Street),
London W8 7LP
Tel: 020 7727 8424

Commemorative ceramics including royal and political subjects.

Jonathan Horne
66c Kensington Church Street,
London W8 4BY
Tel: 020 7221 5658
Fax: 020 7792 3090
www.jonathanhorne.co.uk

Early English pottery, medieval to 1820.

Huxtable's Old Advertising
(ref: Huxtable's)
Alfie's Market,
13–25 Church Street,
London NW8 8DT
Tel: 020 7724 2200

Advertising, collectables, tins, signs, bottles, commemoratives and old packaging from late Victorian.

Jessop Classic Photographica
(ref: Jessop Classic)
67 Great Russell Street,
London WC1
Tel: 020 7831 3640
Fax: 020 7831 3956

Classic photographic equipment, cameras and optical toys.

Kitchen Bygones
13–15 Church Street,
Marylebone,
London NW8 8DT
Tel: 020 7258 3405
Fax: 020 7724 0999

Kitchenalia.

Lacquer Chest, The
(ref: Lacquer Chest)
75 Kensington Church Street,
London W8 4BG
Tel: 020 7937 1306
Fax: 020 7376 0223

Military chests, china, clocks, samplers and lamps.

Langfords Marine Antiques
(ref: Langfords Marine)
The Plaza, 535 Kings Road,
London SW10 0SZ
Tel: 020 7351 4881
Fax: 020 7352 0763
www.langfords.co.uk

Nautical artefacts.

London Antique Gallery
(ref: London Antique)
66e Kensington Church Street,
London W8 4BY
Tel: 020 7229 2934
Fax: 020 7229 2934

Meissen, Dresden, Worcester, Minton, Shelley, Sèvrea, Lalique and bisque dolls.

Mac's Cameras
(ref: Mac's)
262 King Street, Hammersmith,
London W6 0SJ
Tel: 020 8846 9853

Antique camera equipment.

Magpies
152 Wandsworth Bridge Road,
London SW6 2UH
Tel: 020 7736 3738

Small furniture, kitchenware, door furniture, cutlery, lighting, silver and silver-plate.

A. P. Mathews
283 Westbourne Grove,
London W11
Tel: 01622 812590

Antique luggage.

More Than Music Collectables
(ref: More Than Music)
C24–25 Grays Mews Antiques Market,
1–7 Davies Mews,
London W1Y 2LP
Tel: 020 7629 7703
Fax: 01519 565510
www.mtmglobal.com

Rock and popular music memorabilia, specialising in The Beatles.

Directory of Dealers

Murray Cards (International) Ltd
(ref: **Murray Cards**)
51 Watford Way,
London NW4 3JH
Tel: 020 8202 5688
Fax: 020 8203 7878
www.murraycards.com

Cigarette and trade cards

Music & Video Exchange
(ref: **Music & Video**)
38 Notting Hill Gate,
London W11 3HX
Tel: 020 7243 8574
www.mveshops.co.uk

CDs, memorabilia, vinyl – deletions and rarities.

Myriad Antiques
(ref: **Myriad**)
131 Portland Road,
London W11 4LW
Tel: 020 7229 1709
Fax: 020 7221 3882

French painted furniture, garden furniture, bamboo, Victorian and Edwardian upholstered chairs, mirrors and objets d'art.

Colin Narbeth and Son
(ref: **C. Narbeth**)
20 Cecil Court,
London WC2N 4HE
Tel: 020 7379 6975
Fax: 0172 811244
www.colin-narbeth.com

Banknotes, bonds and shares of all countries and periods.

North West Eight
(ref: **North West 8**)
36 Church Street,
London NW8 8EP
Tel: 020 7723 9377

Decorative antiques.

Old School
130c Junction Road,
Tufnell Park,
London N19
Tel: 020 7272 5603

Gardens and interiors.

Old Telephone Company, The
(ref: **Old Telephone Co.**)
The Battlesbridge Antiques Centre,
The Old Granary, Battlesbridge,
Essex SS11 7RE
Tel: 01245 400 601
www.theoldtelephone.co.uk
Antique and collectable telephones.

Pendulum of Mayfair
King House, 51 Maddox Street,
London W1R 9LA
Tel: 020 7629 6606
Fax: 020 7629 6616

Clocks: including longcase, bracket and wall, and Georgian period furniture.

Photographer's Gallery, The
(ref: **Photo. Gallery**)
5 Great Newport Street,
London WC2H 7HY
Tel: 020 7831 1772
Fax: 020 7836 9704
www.photonet.org.uk

Radio Days
87 Lower Marsh,
London SE1 7AB
Tel: 020 7928 0800
Fax: 020 7928 0800

Lighting, telephones, radios, clothing, magazines and cocktail bars from the 1930s–1970s.

Ranby Hall Antiques
(ref: **Ranby Hall**)
Barnby Moor, Retford,
Nottingham DN22 8JQ
Tel: 01777 860696
Fax: 01777 701317
www.ranbyhall.antiques-gb.com

Antiques, decorative items and contemporary objects.

Reel Poster Gallery
(ref: **Reel Poster**)
72 Westbourne Grove,
London W2 5SH
Tel: 020 7727 4488
Fax: 020 7727 4499
www.reelposter.com

Original vintage film posters.

Reel Thing, The
(ref: **Reel Thing**)
17 Royal Opera Arcade, Pall Mall,
London SW1Y 4UY
Tel: 020 7976 1830
Fax: 020 7976 1850
www.reelthing.co.uk

Purveyors of vintage sporting memorabilia.

Retro Exchange
20 Pembridge Road,
London W11
Tel: 020 7221 2055
Fax: 020 7727 4185
www.I/fel.trade.co.uk

Space age-style furniture and 1950's kitsch.

Directory of Dealers

Retro Home
20 Pembridge Road,
London W11
Tel: 020 7221 2055
Fax: 020 7727 4185
www.l/fel.trade.co.uk

Bric-a-brac, antique furniture and objects of desire.

Shahdad Antiques
(ref: Shahdad)
A16–17 Grays-in-Mews,
1–7 Davies Mews,
London W1Y 2LP
Tel: 020 7499 0572
Fax: 020 7629 2176

Islamic and ancient works of art.

Nicholas Shaw Antiques
(ref: N. Shaw)
Great Grooms Antique Centre,
Parbrook, Billinghurst,
West Sussex RH14 9EU
Tel: 01403 786 656
Fax: 01403 786 656
www.nicholas-shaw.com

Scottish and Irish fine silver, small silver and collector's items.

Star Signings
Unit A18–A19 Grays Mews Antiques Market,
1–7 Davies Mews
London W1Y 2LP
Tel: 020 7491 1010
Fax: 020 7491 1070

Sporting autographs and memorabilia.

June & Tony Stone
(ref: J. & T. Stone)
75 Portobello Road,
London W11 2QB
Tel: 020 7221 1121

Fine antique boxes.

Talking Machine, The
30 Watford Way,
London NW4 3AL
Tel: 020 8202 3473
www.gramophones.endirect.co.uk

Mechanical antiques typewriters, radios, music boxes, photographs, sewing machines, juke boxes, calculators and televisions.

Telephone Lines Ltd
(ref: Telephone Lines)
304 High Street, Cheltenham,
Gloucestershire GL50 3JF
Tel: 01242 583699
Fax: 01242 690033
Telephones.

Thimble Society, The
(ref: Thimble Society)
Geoffrey van Arcade, 107 Portobello Road,
London W11 2QB
Tel: 020 7419 9562

Thimbles, sewing items, snuff boxes and lady's accessories.

Sue & Alan Thompson
(ref: S. & A. Thompson)
Highland Cottage, Broomne Hall Road,
Cold Harbour RH5 6HH
Tel: 01306 711970
Fax: 01306 711970

Objects of vertu, antique tortoiseshell items, period furniture and unusual collector's items.

Tredantiques
77 Hill Barton Road, Whipton,
Exeter EX1 3PW
Tel: 01392 447082
Fax: 01392 462200

Furniture.

Trio/Teresa Clayton
(ref: Trio)
L24 Grays Mews Antiques Market,
1–7 Davies Mews,
London W1Y 2LP
Tel: 020 7493 2736
Fax: 020 7493 9344

Perfume bottles and Bohemian glass.

Vintage Wireless Shop
(ref: Vintage Wireless)
The Hewarths Sandiacre,
Nottingham NG10 5NQ
Tel: 0115 939 3139

Radios.

Youll's Antiques
27–28 Charnham Street, Hungerford,
Berkshire RG17 0EJ
Tel: 01488 682046
Fax: 01488 684335
www.youll.com

English/French furniture from seventeenth to twentieth century, porcelain, silver and decorative items.

Index

A

ABC Aerial Gazetteer 16
Accession jug (1837) 34
Accessories, Beatles, official carded 93
Advertising and packaging 11–15
Aerial ABC Gazetteer 16
Aerial timetable 17
Aero Club badge 16
Aeronautica 16–7
Aeroplane cartridge system camera 27
African Republic note 98
Air Force medal 42
Air pageant programme 17
Aircraft of the RAF series cards 48
Aircraft propeller 17
Airplane, model 17
Airship safety award 17
Akira comic 48
Album artwork 95
Aldis slide project 26
Alligator skin bag 69
Amazing Spiderman comic 44
America chess set 32
American "cherries" paperweight 72
American handbag (1940) 68
American handbag (1960) 71
American note ($2) 96
Anatomy of Murder poster 81
Andy and Cow wallpaper limited edition print 79
Andy, Bob & Elvis silver gelatin print 74
Apollo XI potter mug 35
Archive footage, Beatles 92
Arnold Schwin Packard bicycle 18
Art nouveau polyphon 66
Ashtray, Spitfire 104
Asleep on job estate print 76
At Home with Screamin' Jay Hawkins 90
Audioline 310 telephone 108
Austrian 1000 Kronen note 98
Austrian coin 40
Austrian snuff box 105
Autographic camera, Kodak 27

B

Baccarat blue primorose paperweight 72
Baccarat faceted paperweight 73
Baccarat pansy paperweight 73
Baccarat scrambled paperweight 72
Baccarat sulphite paperweight 73
Backgammon and chess set 33

Bad poster 81
Badge, Aero Club 16
Bakelite comb 70
Bakelite pyramid phone 110
Bakelite telephone 107
Bakelite thermos 60
Baker, Shirley, print 77
Baker's paddle 61
Ballerina, musical 65
Bank of England note 99
Barrel decanter 70
Batman comic 49
Batman in the Sixties magazine 47
Battery advertisement, Oldham 13
Bauhaus wooden chess set 31
Beach Boys Album 94
Beaker, golden jubilee (1887) 34
Beano, The comic 50
Bears of Berne wooden chess set 31
Beatles accessories, official carded 93
Beatles archive footage 92
Beatles brooch, official 93
Beatles dress 92
Beatles jewellery box 93
Beatles Parlophone A Label demo 90
Beatles powder compact 89
Beatles series cards 47
Beatles sketch 91
Beatles sneakers 93
Beatles talc powder 92
Beatles Yellow Submarine official toy 93
Beehive 71
Belgian wall telephone 108
Bell & Howell "Sportster Standard 8" cine camera 24
Bell weight 53
Bendix 526C radio 86
Bendorp's cocoa tin 12
Berkel scales 53
Best of the Beach Boys 90
Betacom "Golphone" 108
Bicycles 18
Billiard series cards 44
Billie Bird McVitie biscuit box 13
Biscuit barrel, novelty 56
Biscuit box, Boat 12
Biscuit box, McVitie 13
Biscuit tin 13
Black plastic telephone 111
Blair Stereo Weno camera 29
Blakes 7 magazine 45
Blue primrose paperweight 72
Blue swirl, Clichy paperweight 72
BOAC sales leaflet 16
Boat biscuit box 12
Bobbins (1930) 102
Boer War egg cups 39

Boer War note 97
Bohemian glass pefume bottle 20, 22
Bohemian magnum paperweight 73
Bolex 16mm cine camera 28
Bolex cine camera 26
Bolex Standard cine camera 28
Bolivian note 100
Bolton 1937 silver gelatin print 80
Bond, Brazil railway 99
Bond, Chinese 100
Bond, Portuguese 100
Bond, U.S. railway 99
Bone chess set 33
Bone china jug, royal silver wedding anniversary(1888) 34
Bone china plate, relief of Mafeking 36
Bottle opener 58
Bottle, Broseden 14
Bottle, Swan ink 11
Bottles 19–23
Bourjois Kobako perfume bottle 19
Bournvita mug 14
Box camera, Brownie 26
Box, boat biscuit 12
Box, Lux soap flakes 13
Box, McVitie biscuit 13
Box, Queen of Hearts sweet 12
Boxes, nibs assorted 14
Boxwood and ebony Staunton chess set (19th c) 33
Boxwood and Ebony Staunton chess set 30
Boys' Ranch comic 48
Brandt, Bill, signed print (Nude, London) 79
Brandt, Bill, signed print (Parlour Maid) 79
Brass-mounted photo album 76
Brazil Railway bond 99
Bread bin, enamelled 59
Bread bin, rectangular 57
Bread bin, terracotta 60
Bread knife 56
Brilliantine "Saturday Night Lotion" 14
British Linen Co note 100
Brooch, Beatles official 93
Broseden bottle 14
Brownie 'Flash' camera 27
Brownie box camera 26
Brute Force album 95
Buffy the Vampire Slayer magazine 46
Builders of the British Empire series cards 47
Bush television 87
Bust of Wellington 39

Index

Bust, Queen Elizabeth II 34
Butcher's block (1860) 55
Butcher's block (1890) 58
Butcher's block (1910) 55

C

C8 cine camera, Bolex 28
Cameras 24–9
Candlestick telephone (1916) 110
Candlestick telephone (1927) 110
Canon IV camera 29
Cap badge (Royal Armoured Corps) 42
Cap badge (Royal Sussex Reg) 41
Card case, crocodile skin 68
Card case, mother of pearl 70
Card sign (Kenyon & Cravens) 82
Cards 44, 45
Cards 46, 47
Cards 47, 48, 49
Cards, famous crowns series 43
Cards, Kensitas flower series 43
Cards, Superman series 43
Cards, Titanic series 43
Caricature mug, Thatcher 34
Carpet stitcher 102
Carton, Senior Service cigarettes 14
Cartoon, Ray Lowry 43
Cartoons 44, 45
Cartoons 46
Cartoons 48
Cartridge system camera, aeroplane 27
Carved walking stick 113
Ceramic plaque, George VI coronation 37
Ceramic rolling pin 61
Chamber-stick (1890) 53
Chamber-stick (1910) 57
Charles, Prince, engagement mug 38
Cherries, American paperweight 72
Chess sets 30–33
Chest larder 62
Child's plate, Queen Caroline 39
Children of Nations series cards 48
Children's plate, "England's Hope" 37
Chiming table clock 66
Chinese bond 100
Chinese cash note 97
Chinese sewing box 102
Chinese walking cane 113
Chocolate jug 53
Chocolate tin, Elizabeth II coronation 36
Chopper, herb 54
Churchill toby jug, WInston 35

Cibachrome print 76
Cider jar 62
Cigar box 106
Cigar case, Victorian 68
Cigar cutter 104
Cigarette box 104
Cigarette carton, Senior Service 14
Cigarette sign, Craven "A" 12
Cigarette sign, Wills Star 12
Cigarettes, pack of 71
Cine camera 24
Cine camera 26
Cine camera, Bolex 16mm 28
Cine camera, Meopta 27
Circular mould 62
Circular scent bottle 21
City walking cane 112
CKCO AD75 radio 87
Clear glass scent bottle 23
Clichy blue swirl paperweight 72
Cloche, glass 53
Clock, propellor 70
Cnut, king, silver penny 40
Coalport plate, Victoria diamond jubilee 39
Coca-Cola card sign 81
Cocktail set, Harlequin glass 68
Cocoa tin 57
Cocoa tin, Bendorp's 12
Coins and medals 40–42
Coleman's mustard tins 15
Collar box 64
Colonial note (15s) 96
Colour Fresson print 74
Colour landscape 75
Comb, bakelite 70
Comb, tortoiseshell 69
Comics 43
Comics 44, 45, 46
Comics 48, 49, 50, 52,
Commemorative coin, George VI silver jubilee 40
Commemorative toffee tin, royal wedding 14
Commemorative wear 34–9
Compartmentalised thread box 101
Concert roller organ 67
Concorde postal cover 17
Condom packet 11
Confederates States note 96
Conical perfume bottle 20
Container, "Jolly Baby" talcum powder 13
Continental Film Review magazine (Aug 68) 50
Continental Film Review magazine (Mar 62) 52
Continental vesta case 106
Copper and brass urn 54
Copper funnel 55
Copper jelly moulds 61
Copper jug 58

Copper kettle 57
Cordial syphon 54
Cornish ware mug 59
Coromandel games compendium 32
Coronation (1937) photograph 74
Coronation cup and saucer, Edward VII 39
Coronation cup, Edward VIII 35
Coronation mug, Edward VII 37
Coronation mug, King George V 35
Coronation musical teapot, Elizabeth II 35
Coronet midget roll film camera 25
Costume prints 51
Craven "A" cigarette sign 12
Crawdaddy magazine 51
Cream maker 59
Creamer, glass 59
Cricket ball walking stick 113
Cricket series cards 45
Crimea War medal 41
Crocodile case 63
Crocodile handbag 71
Crocodile skin bag, English 69
Crocodile skin card case 68
Crown coin, George III 40
Crystal set 88
C-type colour print 74
C-type print (Girl in hammock) 76
C-type print (Hot Dandelion) 80
C-type print (Jason Oddy) 78
C-type print (Nigel Shafran) 78
C-type print (Soccer Wonderland) 75
C-type print, limited edition (Edie Sedgwick) 79
C-type print, signed (Hulme) 75
C-type print, signed (Kitchen sink) 78
C-type print, signed (Lina) 75
C-type print, signed (Monroe) 77
Cup and saucer, Edward VII coronation 39
Cup, loving, Margaret Thatcher 38
Curse of Frankenstein poster 82
Custard drawing 48
Cyanotype photograph 74
Cylinder piano 65
Cypher, victoria 38

D

Dandy comic 45
Danish telephone (1930) 108
Danish telephone (1935, D30 variation) 109
Danish telephone (1935,

Index

magneto) 107
Daredevil comic 49
Darth Vader telephone 109
Dean, James, silver gelatin print 77
Deardoff field camera 24
Decanter, barrel 70
Delft plaque, liberation of Holland 36
Desk telephone (1895) 111
Desk telephone (1960) 109
Diaboliques, Les poster 85
Dog food sign, Spratt 15
Dog model gramophone 67
Donna Che Visse due Volte, La poster 85
Double snuff box 106
Dr Who Annual, The 50
Dresden porcelain figurine 11
Dress, Beatles 92

E

Eales cartoon 45
Edie Sedgwick limited edition print 79
Edward VII coronation cup and saucer 39
Edward VII coronation mug 37
Edward VII, letter from 97
Edward VIII coronation loving cup 35
Edwardian shop scales 69
Egg cups, Boer War 39
Egg cups, novelty 56
Egg timer 60
Ekco model TA201 television 87
Elephant walking cane 113
Elizabeth II coronation chocolate tin 36
Elizabeth II coronation musical teapot 35
Elizabeth II silver jubilee Poole pottery vase 35
Elvis 68 – 91
Elvis Presley telephone 107
Embossed tin sign 82
Emersa radio 86
Enamel scent bottle 21
Engagement mug, Prince Charles 38
England 1966 squad photograph 97
England's Hope children's plate 37
English gramophone 67
English note 99
English scent bottle 23
Ephemera 43–52
Ericofon telephone 110
Ericsson telephone 111
Estate print (Asleep on job) 76
Eye glass 69

F

F For Fake poster 85
Faceted baccarat paperweight 73
Fada streamliner radio 86
Famous crowns series cards 43
Famous Film scenes series cards 46
Famous Monsters comic 47
Fan and humidifier 69
Fantastic Four comic 44
Faventia Spanish street piano 67
Field camera 26
Field camera, Deardoff 24
Fifty 50 mark note 98
Fighter plane model, Tornado 16
Figure, Robertson's Golly Lollipop Man 15
Figurine, Dresden porcelain 11
Fijian treasury note 99
Film Fun cartoon 47
Filma projector 24
Fish kettle (1880) 57
Fish kettle (1900) 54
500 rouble note 97
500 series telephone 108
Five Reichsmark note 98
Flash-bulb holder 25
Flask, food storage 61
Flat iron 54
Floral St Louis paperweight 73
Flour jar 58
Flour tin 58
Flower series cards, Kensitas 43
Folly, pottery 39
Food storage flask 61
Forte Piano musical box 66
4AD calendar 95, Harrison, George, autobiography 92
Four castles plate 36
French apothecary's bottles 20
French ivory chess set (1800) 33
French ivory chess set (1845) 30
French photograph album 74
Fresson print, colour 74
Funnel, copper 55
Funnel, metal 61

G

GEC radio 86
Gelatin print, signed (Ringo) 75
Genie telephone 110
Gent magazine 51
George III crown coin 40
George III half-sovereign coin 40
George IV snuff box 106
George V coronation whisky decanter 37
George V letter from 98
George V silver jubilee mug 38
George V, King, coronation mug 35
George VI coronation ceramic plaque 37
George VI coronation wedgwood mug 37
George VI silver jubilee commemorative coin 40
German chess set 32
Get Carter poster 83
Gimme Shelter poster 84
Girl in hammock C-type print 76
Gladstone Travelling bag 64
Glass cloche 53
Glass creamer 59
Goat head snuff box 104
Gold and tortoiseshell snuff box 105
Gold guinea coin, Edward III (1794) 40
Gold guinea coin, Edward III (1813) 40
Gold sovereign coin, Queen Mary 40
Golden jubilee beaker (1887) 34
Golden jubilee mug (1887) 34
Goldfinger poster 81
Golphone, Betacom 108
Graduate, The poster 85
Gramophone, dog model 67
Gramophone, English 67
Gramophone, portable 65
Great War medal 41
Great War memorial plaque 42
Green jasper paperweight 72
Green scent bottle 23
Grille radio 88
Grossmith "Old Cottage" Lavender Water bottle 20
Guerlain "L'Heure Bleue" perfume bottle 20
Guinea coin, gold, Edward III (1794) 40
Guinea coin, gold, Edward III (1813) 40
Guinness print 12
Guinness toucan stand 15
Guinness toucan tray 15
Gun case 64

H

Hair grip 69
Half-sovereign coin, George III 40
Handbag, American (1940) 68
Handbag, American (1960) 71
Handbag, crocodile 71
Handbag, lizard skin 71
Handbag, poodle 71
Hardwood sewing box 103
Hardy, Bert, silver gelatin print 78
Harlequin glass cocktail set 68
Hat box 63 64
Hat case, Victorian 63
Heart-shaped perfume bottle 20, 22

122

Index

Heavy Metal magazine 92
Hepburn, signed Bob Willoughby print 77
Herb chopper 54
Hexagonal mould 62
Hoffman Suisse book biscuit tin 13
Holliday, signed Bob Willoughby print 77
Hollywood splicer 25
Hoof walking cane 112
Hopkins, John, print 80
Horlicks glass jug 13
Horn snuff mull 104
Hot Dandelion C-type print 80
Houghton Ticka spy camera 29
Hulme, signed C-type print 75
Humber gents bicycle 18
Hungarian pengo note 97

I

I Me Mine, George Harrison autobiography 92
Ian Macdonald print 78
Incredible Hulk comic 44
Incredible Hulk comic 49
Ink bottle, Swan 11
Ink filler 62
Inlaid sewing box 103
Intercom speaker 86
International Times magazine 52
Interview magazine 52
Invicta Table TL5 television 88
Iraqi note 100
Irish bank note 100
Iron Maiden picture disc 91
Iron, flat 54
Ivory chess set, French (1800) 33
Ivory chess set, French (1845) 30
Ivory chess set, Russian 31
Ivory monobloc chess set 31
Ivory telephone 109

J

James Dean silver gelatin print 77
Japanese walking cane 112
Jar, flour 58
Jar, marmalade 56
Jasper, green paperweight 72
Jelly moulds, copper 61
Jess Il Bandito poster 83
Jewellery box, Beatles, official carded 93
John Bull Tyres manufacturers sign 11
John Lennon mug 90
John's Children 91
Jolly Baby talcum powder container 13
Jour de Fête poster 84
Jug, accession (1837) 34
Jug, chocolate 53
Jug, copper 58
Jug, water 57
Jug, Winston Churchill toby 35
Jug-shaped ruby scent bottle 22
Jungle Book poster 81
JVC television 88

K

KB wooden radio 87
Kensitas flower series cards 43
Kettle, copper 57
Key rings, motoring 15
King George V coronation mug 35
Kingswood sewing box 103
Kitchen sink signed C-type print 78
Kitchenalia 53–61
Knebworth Park programme 91
Knife sharpener 54
Knife, bread 56
Kodak autographic camera 27
Kodak field camera 24
Kodak Medallist II camera 28
Kodak Retina IIF camera 29
Konga comic 49
Kophot light exposure meter 26

L

Land Rover series cards 49
Larder chest 62
Lartique print 77
Latissimo glass perfume bottle 19
Le Mans poster 83
Leather trunk 63
Lecoultre musical box 66
Legnano lady's bicycle 18
Leica 35mm SLR camera 24
Leica Chico flash-bulb holder 25
Leicaflex SLR camera 25
Lennon, John, mug 90
Leopold II medal 42
Letter from King Edward VII 97
Letter from King George V 98
Letter opener, tortoiseshell 68
Liberation of Holland Delft plaque 36
Light exposure meter 26
Limited edition C-type print (Edie Sedgwick) 79
Limited edition print (Andy and Cow wallpaper) 79
Lina, signed C-type print 75
Little Comfort small sewing machine 101
Lizard skin handbag 71
Lone Ranger, The comic 52
Loving cup, Edward VIII coronation 35
Loving cup, Margaret Thatcher 38
Loving cup, Victoria diamond jubilee 36
Lowry, Ray, cartoon 43
Lucas, Cornel 80
Luftwaffe Eigentum robot camera 26
Luggage 63–4
Lux soap flakes box 13

M

Macdonald, Ian, print 78
Macintosh toffee tin, commemorative 14
Mad Monsters comic 50
Madonna single 89
Magazines 45, 46, 47
Magazines 50, 51
Magazines 50, 51, 52
Magical World of Disney series cards 49
Magneto telephone 109
Magnum, Bohemian paperweight 73
Mahogany snuff box 105
Maidens… silver gelatin print 74
Mail bag 64
Mains radio 88
Mamiya 120 camera 25
Manic Street Preachers single (1988) 94
Manic Street Preachers single (1990) 89
Manufacturer's sign, John Bull Tyres 11
Map, Qantas Empire Airways 16
Marconi mastergram 87
Margaret Thatcher caricature mug 34
Margaret Thatcher loving cup 38
Markers, trumps 15
Marmalade jar 56
Marvel Masterworks comic 45
Mary, Queen, gold sovereign 40
Masterworks, Marvel comic 45
Match strike 104
Matthew Murray print 77
Mayfair magazine 46
Mazarin blue glass perfume bottle 19
Mechanical music 65–8
Medals and coins 40–42
Meek, Joe, portrait by 92
Memorabilia, Siouxsie and the Banshees 94
Memorial plaque, Great war 42
Meopta cine camera 27
Metal funnel 61
Mickey Mouse camera 27
Mighty Thor comic 52
Military chess set 32
Military clasp 42
Military guinea coin 40
Military medal trio 42
Military payment note (10¢) 96

123

Index

Milk churn 70
Milton Keynes signed sliver gelatin print 79
Miners' strike plate 38
Mini sweeper 59
Miniature medals 41
Miniature musical box 65
Miniature Singer sewing machine 102
Miniature spy camera, Minox B 25
Minox B miniature spy camera 25
Miscellaneous 68–71
Model 1000 telephone 110
Model airplane 17
Model kit, "Robot Bomb" 16
Model, Tornado fighter plane 16
Mojo magazine (No. 24 blue) 91
Mojo magazine (No. 24 red) 90
Monkey snuff box 104
Monroe, signed C-type print 77
Monsieur Plitt... silver gelatin print 74
Monte Hale comic 44
Mortar & pestle 56
Mother of pearl card case 70
Motoring key rings 15
Mould, circular 62
Mould, hexagonal 62
Movie cameraman... silver gelatin print 80
MPP micro precision field camera 26
Mug, Bournvita 14
Mug, Cornish ware 59
Mug, coronation Edward VII 37
Mug, George V silver jubilee 38
Mug, golden jubilee (1887) 34
Mug, John Lennon 90
Mug, King George V coronation 35
Mug, Ovaltine 58
Mug, Prince Charles engagement 38
Mug, Royal Doulton (pilot) 68
Mug, Victorian, Royal visit 36
Mug, wedgwood, George VI coronation 37
Murray, Matthew print 77
Music Star magazine 52
Musical ballerina 65
Musical box (1865) 66
Musical box (1895) 66
Musical box Lecoultre 66
Musical box, Forte Piano 66
Musical box, miniature 65
Musical box, Swiss 65
Musical box, twelve air 65
Musical decanter 66
Musical teapot, Elizabeth II coronation 35
Mustard tins, Coleman's 15
Mythological chess set 30

N

National costumes series cards 46
National Currency $20 note 96
Necessaire, tortoiseshell and silver 102
Needle case (1890) 101
New Orleans $20 note 96
Nib boxes, assortment 14
Nina Ricci "Coeur-Joie" perfume bottle 20
North Islands... silver gelatin print 78
Notable MPs series cards 48
Noted Cats series cards 48
Novelty biscuit barrel 56
Novelty egg cups 56
Novelty vesta case 105
Nude, London signed Bill Brandt print 79
Nude... signed gelatin print 76

O

Observer, The cartoon 46
Oddy, Jason, C-type print 78
Officer on horseback 36
Oldham battery advertisement 13
Opaque scent bottle, silver-topped 23
Opera series cards 44
Order of the Indian Empire (1900) 41
Organette 67
Oval scent bottle 21
Ovaltine mug 58

P

Painted metal chess set 30
Pansy, baccarat paperweight 73
Paper money & Scripophilly 96–100
Paperweights 72–3
Paris print 76
Parlour Maid signed Bill Brandt print 79
Paul Ysart paperweight 72
Penny, silver, King Cnut 40
Perfume flasks, royal wedding (1840) 37, 39
Perfume/scent bottles 19–23
Perpetual calendar 70
Philips radio 88
Phonograph (1900) 66
Phonograph cylinders 67
Photograph album, brass-mounted 76
Photograph album, French 74
Photograph, England 1966 squad 97
Photographs 74–80
Piano, cylinder 65
Picnic case 63
Picnic hamper 63

Pie funnel 53
Plane model, Tornado fighter 16
Planet of the Apes poster 83
Plaque, ceramic, George VI coronation 37
Plaque, liberation of Holland 36
Plaque, memorial, great war 42
Plaque, Wedgwood paperweight 73
Plate, "England's Hope" children's 37
Plate, child's, Queen Caroline 39
Plate, coalport, Victoria diamond jubilee 39
Plate, four castles 36
Plate, miners' strike 38
Plate, relief of Mafeking bone china 36
Playboy magazine 45
Police singles box 94
Political cartoon 44
Polyphon Style 45, table model 65
Polyphon Style 48, table model 67
Polyphon, art nouveau 66
Poodle handbag 71
Poole pottery vase, Elizabeth II silver jubilee 35
Porcelain figurine, Dresden 11
Portable gramophone 65
Portable radio 88
Portrait by Joe Meek 92
Portuguese bond 100
Portuguese European v Chinese chess set (l. 19th c) 30
Postal cover, Concorde 17
Posters 81–3
Potato cutter 59
Potato masher 60
Pottery folly 39
Pottery mug, Apollo XI 35
Powder compact (Beatles) 89
Presley, Elvis, telephone 107
Prince Charles engagement mug 38
Prince Matchabello "Beloved" perfume bottle 19
Prints 51
Programme, Air pageant 17
Projector, Filma 24
Promotional magazine, Whitehead aircraft 17
Propeller clock 70
Przygoda L'Avventura poster 84
Pseudonym Autonym poster 82
Psycho poster 83
Purma rolla camera 25
Pyramid tripod 26

Q

Qantas Empire Airways map 16
Quarter-plate camera 27

Index

Quartz chess set 31
Que Viva Mexiko poster 84
Queen Caroline child's plate 39
Queen Elizabeth II bust 34
Queen Mary gold sovereign 40
Queen of Hearts sweet box 12
Queen's Silver Jubilee telephone 110

R

R2D2 telephone 108
Radio Times cartoon 46
Radio, TV & sound equipment 86–8
Railroad share certificate 99
Railway bond, Brazil 99
Railway bond, U.S. 99
Raleigh Roadster bicycle 18
Raleigh Rocky II bicycle 18
Rangefinder camera, Kodak 28
Rebellion/Bunt poster 84
Rectangular bread bin 57
Red glass scent bottle 22
Reflex camera 24
Regency sewing box 103
Regency table cabinet 101
Reine de Joie poster 83
Relief of Mafeking bone china plate 36
Ringo, signed gelatin print 75
Rival (Norwich) lady's bicycle 18
Robertson's Golly Lollipop Man figure 15
Robot Bomb model kit 16
Robot camera 26
Robotech comic 50
Rock and pop 89–95
Roll camera, Purma 25
Roll film camera, Coronet midget 25
Rollei 35 camera, 29
Rollei 35 camera, with box 29
Rollei camera 24
Roller organ, concert 67
Rollerflex reflex camera 24
Rolling pin 60
Rolling pin, ceramic 61
Rolling Stone magazine 51
Rolling Stones album (1971, *Sticky Fingers*) 95
Rolling Stones album (1971, *Stone Age*) 89
Rolling Stones album (1975) 90
Romantic Story comic 44
Roses series cards 48
Rosewood sewing box 103
Royal Doulton mug (pilot) 68
Royal visit teapot 38
Royal visit Victorian mug 36
Royal wedding perfume flasks (1840) 37, 39
Ruby scent bottle, jug-shaped 22
Russian ivory chess set 31
Russian medal (1915) 41
Russian note 99
Russian walking cane 113

S

St Louis floral paperweight 73
St Louis paperweight 72
Sales leaflet, BOAC 16
Salt cellar, Sifta 12
Salt tin 54
Saturday Night Lotion, Brilliantine 14
Saucepot, brass 62
Saville London "June" perfume bottle 19
Scales, Berkel 53
Scales, Edwardian shop 69
Scales, Royal 57
Scales, Swedish 62
Scent/perfume bottles 19–23
Schaparelli perfume bottle 19
Scottish pound note 100
Scrambled, baccarat paperweight 72
Scripophily & paper money 96–100
Searle Lithograph 44
Selenus chess set 30
Senior Service cigarette carton 14
Series 700 telephone 107
Sewing basket (early 19th century) 102
Sewing box (1800) 102
Sewing box, Chinese 102
Sewing box, hardwood 103
Sewing box, inlaid 103
Sewing box, Kingswood 103
Sewing box, Regency 103
Sewing box, rosewood 103
Sewing box, sycamore 103
Sewing companion 101
Sewing items 101–3
Sewing machine, small (Little Comfort) 101
Sewing table (1840) 101
Shadow Hawk comic 52
Shafran, Nigel, C-type print 78
Share certificate, railroad 99
Share certificate, signed U.S. 99
Shirley Baker print 77
Shirt-sleeve board 62
Shop scales, Edwardian 69
Shop sign 11
Showcard 82
Siege of Khartoum note 97
Sifta salt cellar 12
Sifter, sugar 61
Sign, Spratt dog food 15
Signed Bob Willoughby print (Hepburn) 77
Signed Bob Willoughby print (Holliday) 77
Signed C-type print (Hulme) 75
Signed C-type print (Kitchen sink) 78
Signed C-type print (Lina) 75
Signed C-type print (Monroe) 77
Signed gelatin print (Nude…) 76
Signed gelatin print (Ringo) 75
Signed gelatin print (swimming pool) 75
Signed print (Snow drops 2000) 80
Signed silver gelatin print (Milton Keynes) 79
Signed U.S. share certificate 99
Silver chess set 33
Silver gelatin print (Andy, Bob & Elvis) 74
Silver gelatin print (Bert Hardy) 78
Silver gelatin print (Bolton 1937) 80
Silver gelatin print (James Dean) 77
Silver gelatin print (Maidens…) 74
Silver gelatin print (Monsieur Plitt…) 74
Silver gelatin print (Movie cameraman…) 80
Silver gelatin print (North Islands…) 78
Silver gelatin print (The Popes…) 80
Silver gelatin print (untitled Humphrey Spender) 77
Silver gelatin print (Vali reflected…) 76
Silver gelatin print, signed (Milton Keynes) 79
Silver gilt snuff box 105
Silver Jubilee mug, George V 38
Silver penny, King Cnut 40
Silver scent bottle 19
Silver taper 106
Silver thimbles 103
Silver Tone Bullet radio 87
Silver vesta case 105
Silver-topped scent bottle 23
Singer sewing machine, miniature 102
Sink, stone 53
Siouxsie and the Banshees memorabilia 94
Sketch, Beatles 91
Sleeping Beauty poster 83
Slide projector, Aldis 26
SLR camera, Leica 35 mm 24
SLR camera, Leicaflex 25
Small sewing machine (Little Comfort) 101
Smoking equipment 104–6
Snakewood walking cane 112
Sneakers, Beatles 93
Snow drops 2000 signed print 80

Index

Snuff boxes 104–6
Snuffbox, Victorian 35
Soccer Wonderland print 75
Soho International magazine 45
Sonorette radio 86
Spadge guinea coin 40
Spanish airline leaflet 16
Spender, Humphrey silver gelatin print (untitled) 79
Spiderman, Amazing comic 44
Spitfire ashtray 104
Splicer, Hollywood 25
Sportster cine camera 24
Spratt dog food sign 15
Springs cartoon 44
Springsteen, Bruce, single 94
Spy camera, Houghton Ticka 29
Spy camera, miniature 25
Squad photograph, England 97
Square roll film camera 27
Stand-up card sign 81
Star Trek comic 43
Star Wars poster 82
Staunton chess set 30, 31, 33
Stoneware bottle, Whit 23
Strange Tales comic 43
Strange Tales comic 45
Strawbs album 89
Street piano 67
Studio International Art magazine 47
Sturbridge paperweight 73
Sueurs Froides poster 85
Sugar sifter 61
Suitcases 63
Sulphite paperweight 73
Sunday Times, The cartoon 48
Superman series cards 43
Swan ink bottle 11
Swedish kronor note 98
Sweet box, Queen of Hearts 12
Swimming pool signed gelatin print 75
Swiss musical box 65
Swiss note 100
Swiss telephone 107
Sycamore sewing box 103
Syphon, cordial 54

T

Table clock, chiming 66
Table model Style 45 polyphon 65
Table model Style 48 polyphon 67
Talc powder, Beatles 92
Talcum powder container, "Jolly Baby" 13
Teapot (1930) 55
Teapot (1932) 56
Teapot, royal visit 38
Teapot, Victoria diamond jubilee 37

Teleca Bino camera 28
Telephones 107–111
TV/radio & gramophone 87
The Popes... silver gelatin print 80
Thermos, bakelite 60
Thimbles, silver 103
35mm SLR camera, Leica 24
Thor comic 43
Thornton Pickard camera 28
Thread box 101
300 series telephone 108-111
Three pence note 97
Tibetan note 98
Tin, cocoa 57
Tin, flour 58
Tin, Hoffman Suisse biscuit 13
Tin, salt 54
Tins, Coleman's mustard 15
Titanic series cards 43
Toasters 55, 58
Toby jug, Winston Churchill 35
Toothpaste tub, Woods 13
Top hat and box 64
Tornado fighter plane model 16
Tortoiseshell & ivory chess set 30
Tortoiseshell and silver necessaire 102
Tortoiseshell comb 69
Tortoiseshell letter opener 68
Travelling trunk 64
Trays, Guinness 15
Trimphone 109
Trumps markers 15
Truncheon, World War I 71
Trunk, leather 63
Tunbridge ware sewing companion 101
Turtle Diary poster 85
2001: A Space Odyssey poster 81

U

U.S. Railway bond 99
U.S. share certificate, signed 99
U2 helmet 89
U2 single 89
Ugandan bank note 98
Un Homme et une Femme poster 82
Untied Diaries boxed set 92
Upright dial telephone 107
Urn, copper and brass 54

V

Vali reflected... silver gelatin print 76
Vase, Elizabeth II silver jubilee Poole pottery 35
Verve, The 91
Vesta cases 105, 106
Viaggio in Italia poster 84
Victoria diamond jubilee coalport plate 39
Victoria diamond jubilee loving cup 36
Victoria diamond jubilee teapot 37
Victorian cigar case 68
Victorian Cypher 38
Victorian mug, Royal visit 36
Victorian scent bottles 21, 23
Victorian snuff box 35, 106
Viscount telephone 107
Vogue magazine 47

W

Walking sticks 112–3
Wall telephone, Belgian 108
Watchmen comic 46
Water jug 57
Watering cans (1860) 56
Watering can (1880) 55
Waterloo medal 42
Waterloo series cards 49
Wedgwood mug, George VI coronation 37
Wedgwood plaque paperweight 73
Wellington bust 39
Whalebone cane 112
Whisky decanter, George V coronation 37
Whit stoneware bottle 23
Whitehead aircraft promotional magazine 17
Who, The, album 93
Widelux camera 28
Willoughby, Bob, print, signed (Hepburn) 77
Willoughby, Bob, print, signed (Holliday) 77
Wills Star cigarette sign 12
Wings album 90
Wings record sleeve 90
Winston Churchill toby jug 35
Witchblade comic 47
Wooden cane 112
Work table, Scandinavian 101
World War I truncheon 71

X

X-Men comic 46

Y

Yellow Submarine official Beatles toy 93
Ysart, Paul paperweight 72

Z

Zeta magazine 51
Zig Zag magazine 50
Zomp! Magazine 51

Notes

Notes

MEASUREMENT CONVERSION CHART

This chart provides a scale of measurements converted from centimetres and metres to feet and inches.

1cm	$\frac{2}{5}$in
2cm	$\frac{4}{5}$in
3cm	$1\frac{1}{10}$in
4cm	$1\frac{3}{5}$in
5cm	2in
10cm	$3\frac{7}{8}$in
15cm	$5\frac{9}{10}$in
20cm	$7\frac{3}{4}$in
25cm	$9\frac{4}{5}$in
30cm	$11\frac{4}{5}$in
40cm	1ft $3\frac{3}{4}$in
50cm	1ft $7\frac{2}{3}$in
75cm	2ft $5\frac{1}{2}$in
1 m	3ft $3\frac{1}{3}$in
1.25m	4ft $1\frac{1}{5}$in
1.5m	4ft 11in
1.75m	5ft $8\frac{9}{10}$in
2m	6ft $6\frac{3}{4}$in
2.25m	7ft $4\frac{3}{5}$in
2.5m	8ft $2\frac{2}{5}$in
3m	9ft $10\frac{1}{10}$in